SIGNPOSTS
FOR THE FUTURE

HANS KÜNG

SIGNPOSTS FOR THE FUTURE

1978

DOUBLEDAY & COMPANY, INC.

GARDEN CITY, NEW YORK

Library of Congress Cataloging in Publication Data

Küng, Hans, 1928–
  Signposts for the future.

  Collection of articles translated from the German.
  Includes bibliographical references.
  1. Catholic Church—Doctrinal and controversial works—Catholic authors—
Addresses, essays, lectures.
  I. Title.
  BX1756.K85S57   230′.2
  ISBN: 0-385-13151-8
  Library of Congress Catalog Card Number 77-75387

1121

Grateful acknowledgment is given for permission to include excerpts from
the following copyrighted publications:
  ON BEING A CHRISTIAN: TWENTY THESES was originally published in German
under the title 20 THESEN ZUM CHRISTSEIN (© R. Piper & Co. Verlag, Munich,
1975).
  THE CHRISTIAN IN SOCIETY was originally published in German under the
title DER CHRIST IN DER GESELLSCHAFT: EIN GESPRÄCH (© Ex Libris, Zurich,
1975).
  JESUS IN CONFLICT: A JEWISH-CHRISTIAN DIALOGUE was originally published
in German under the title JESUS IM WIDERSTREIT: EIN JÜDISCH-CHRISTLICHER
Dialog (© Calwer Verlag, Stuttgart, and Kösel-Verlag, Munich, 1976).
  AN ECUMENICAL INVENTORY was originally published in German as an article
in Meyers Enzyklopädisches Lexikon under the title KATHOLISCH–EVANGELISCH:
EINE ÖKUMENISCHE BESTANDSAUFNAHME (© Bibliographisches Institut, Mann-
heim/Vienna/Zurich).
  PATIENTLY STANDING HIS GROUND was originally published in German under
the title GEDULDIG SEINEN PLATZ BEHAUPTEN (© Lutherische Monatsheft,
1975).
  WORSHIP TODAY—WHY? was originally published in German in the series
Theologische Meditationen as GOTTESDIENST—WARUM? (© Benziger Verlag,
Zurich/Einsiedeln/Cologne, 1976).
  WHAT IS CONFIRMATION? was originally published in German in the series
Theologische Meditationen as WAS IST FIRMUNG (© Benziger Verlag, Zurich/
Einsiedeln/Cologne, 1976).
  TRIBUTE TO KARL BARTH by Hans Küng, translated by James Biechler, from
Journal of Ecumenical Studies, Vol. 6, No. 2. Copyright © 1969 by Temple
University Press. Reprinted by permission of Journal of Ecumenical Studies.

*230.2
K 96 s*

CONTENTS

PREFACE

There are many dimensions to being a Christian. It is one and the same Christian who lives in the Church and in society, who lives and works together with Jews, with Christians of other denominations, and with non-Christians. Being a Christian means also constant adaptation to different spheres of life.

In my book *On Being a Christian* I tried to lay the theological foundations: What is the distinctive feature of Christianity? Who is Christ? Who is a Christian? Who acts as a Christian? It was only after I had worked on this large book that I could venture to produce a synthesis of what being a Christian means today. The result is to be found in "Twenty Theses," which I have tried out before large and small audiences from Helsinki and Munich to Cambridge and Washington. These theses are now being eagerly studied in different countries, not only by individuals but also by small groups in schools and parishes. The discussion "The Christian in Society" may be used as a complement to the theses.

It was also only after the book *On Being a Christian* that I was able to enter into a discussion with a Jewish theologian which did not cover merely the usual topics of anti-Semitism, human rights, and other cultural and religious common interests but dealt with the intrinsic difference: the Jew Jesus of Nazareth, who for Christians is the Christ. This discussion, "Jesus in Conflict," was not first written out in an academic fashion but took place "live" as a radio broadcast.

The ecumenical dialogue with Jews is comparatively new to me, but I have been involved in the dialogue between *Catholics and Protestants* from the time when I began work on my dissertation for the doctorate on the great Protestant theologian Karl Barth, which was first published in 1957. It was a great honor for me to be the only Catholic theologian to speak in the Minster at Basel at the memorial service after his death in 1968 ("Tribute to Karl Barth"). The progress in ecumenical understanding achieved since then—especially through the Second Vatican Council—can be seen in "An Ecumenical Inventory." These achievements must not be forgotten in the midst of the present stagnation in the Catholic Church.

I am sure that we can go further also in the difficult questions which remain, especially in practice. The chapters "What Is the Essence of Apostolic Succession?" and "Pro Intercommunion" show that from a theological standpoint there is nothing to prevent either intercommunion or the recognition of the ministries of the Orthodox, Anglican, or Protestant churches. What is necessary is that pope and bishops should finally take note of the theological studies of recent years and draw the appropriate practical conclusions. In any case the important thing today is for the theologian in particular not to adopt an attitude of resignation but, without any sort of opportunism, to continue "Patiently Standing His Ground."

Undoubtedly the Christian churches today and especially the *Catholic Church* have many problems, tensions, polarizations. One often wonders how conservatives and progressives can stay in the same church without splitting up into different parties. The attempt has been made here to take a realistic view of the situation, to provide a theological clarification, and to suggest practical solutions: not only for the problem of "Parties in the Church," but also for the "Participation of the Laity in Church Leadership and in Church Elections" —a central problem for the renewal of the Catholic Church today.

In this connection the question of women really amounts to a test case of readiness for renewal in the Church and for ecumenical agreement. After the latest theologically impoverished Roman document against the ordination of women, I find no reason to change anything in the sixteen theses on "Women in Church and Society" which appeared a short time before it in the New York *Times*.

I am particularly worried by the problem of *worship* in the Church, at a time when attendance has declined, one might say, dramatically even in the United States. Many are asking: "What is the point of worship today?" They will find an answer here ("Worship Today—Why?") on the lines which I worked out in a lecture to the Thomas More Society in Chicago and on other occasions. I would have preferred to deal with all questions concerning worship in my book on the sacraments which I planned a long time ago. But since this has been held up by my work on the questions of Christ and of God, I decided to put forward some ideas here both on the urgent questions of worship and on the no-less-urgent question of *confirmation* in the Catholic Church ("What Is Confirmation?").

Many of the demands made in this volume may sound illusory. This does not make them any the less justified. Even before the Council much that seemed to stem from an illusion had to be demanded and now, after the Council, is part of the everyday routine of Christians. In the present situation of the Church, therefore, the important thing for lay people and theologians is to keep up their courage and work for the future. Perhaps we need a new ecumenical council, perhaps a more effective synod of bishops, or perhaps only a new pontificate, so that we can get away from the present impasse in the Catholic Church and in the ecumenical movement and produce the solutions which have been obvious for a long time to many at the grass-roots level. These *Signposts for the Future* are intended not merely to show the direction but also to keep hope alive.

HANS KÜNG

Tübingen, Pentecost 1977

PART ONE

ON BEING A CHRISTIAN
Twenty Theses

1. No one is a Christian simply because he or she tries to live in a human or in a social or even in a religious way. That person alone is a Christian who tries to live his or her human, social, and religious life in the light of Jesus Christ.
2. The distinctive Christian reality is Jesus Christ himself.
3. Being a Christian means: By following Jesus Christ, the human being in the world of today can truly humanly love, act, suffer, and die, in happiness and unhappiness, life and death, sustained by God and helpful to men.

4. The Christ is no other than the historical Jesus of Nazareth. Neither priest nor political revolutionary, neither ascetic monk nor devout moralist, he is provocative on all sides.
5. Jesus did not proclaim any theological theory or any new law, nor did he proclaim himself. He proclaimed the kingdom of God: God's cause (= God's will), which will prevail and which is identical with man's cause (= man's well-being).
6. For the sake of men's well-being Jesus effectively relativized sacred institutions, law, and cult.
7. Jesus thus asserted a claim to be advocate of God and men. He provoked a final decision: not for a particular title, a dogma, or law but for his good news. But in this way, too, the question of his person was indirectly raised: heretical teacher, false prophet, blasphemer, seducer of the people—or what?
8. In the last resort the conflict centers on God. Jesus does not invoke a new God. He invokes the God of Israel—understood in a new way, as Father of the abandoned, whom he addresses quite personally as his Father.

9. Jesus' violent end was the logical consequence of this approach of his to God and man. His violent passion was the reaction of the guardians of the law, justice, and morality to his nonviolent action: the crucifixion becomes the fullfillment of the curse of the law; Jesus becomes the representative of lawbreakers, of sinners. He dies forsaken by both men and God.

10. Jesus' death, however, was not the end of everything. The faith of his community is: The Crucified is living forever with God, as our hope. Resurrection does not mean either a return to life in space and time or a continuation of life in space and time but the assumption into that incomprehensible and comprehensive last and first reality which we call God.

11. The resurrection faith, therefore, is not an appendage but a radicalizing of faith in God: of faith in God the Creator.

12. Without faith in the risen Christ, faith in the crucified Jesus lacks confirmation and authorization. Without faith in the cross, faith in the risen Christ lacks its distinctive character and decisiveness. The ultimate distinctive feature of Christianity is Jesus Christ as the Crucified.

13. The emergence of the Church can be explained only in the light of faith in Jesus raised to life: the Church of Jesus Christ as the community of those who have committed themselves to the cause of Jesus Christ and bear witness to it as hope for all men.

14. The essential distinction between "Catholic" and "Protestant" today no longer lies in particular doctrinal differences but in the diversity of basic attitudes which have developed since the Reformation but which can now be overcome in their one-sidedness and integrated into a true ecumenicity.

15. The ecumenical basis of all Christian churches is the biblical profession of faith in Jesus as the Christ, as the criterion for man's relations with God and with his fellow men. This profession of faith must be freshly translated for each new age.

C. Who acts as a Christian?   31

16. The distinctive feature of Christian action, therefore, is the following of Christ. This Jesus Christ is in person the living, archetypal embodiment of his cause: embodiment of a new attitude to life and a new way of life. As a concrete, historical person, Jesus Christ possesses an impressiveness, audibility, and realizability

which is missing in an eternal idea, an abstract principle, a universal norm, a conceptual system.

17. Jesus then means for modern man a basic model of a view of life and practice of life to be realized in many ways. Both positively and negatively he is in person invitation ("you may"), appeal ("you should"), challenge ("you can"), for the individual and society. He makes possible in the concrete a new basic orientation and basic attitude, new motivations, dispositions, projects, a new background of meaning and a new objective.

18. For the Church, too, Jesus must remain the authoritative standard in all things. The Church is credible only when it follows in his way as a provisional, serving, guilty, determined Church. At all times practical consequences must be drawn from this for constant internal church reform and for ecumenical understanding.

19. It is particularly in coping with the negative side of life that Christian faith and non-Christian humanisms have to face their acid test. For the Christian the only appropriate way to cope with the negative is in the light of the cross. Following the cross does not mean cultic adoration, mystical absorption, or ethical imitation. It means practice in a variety of ways in accordance with the cross of Jesus, in which a person freely perceives and attempts to follow his own way of life and suffering.

20. Yet, despite all demands for action, looking to the crucified Jesus, the ultimately important thing for man will not be his achievements (justification by works), but his absolute trust in God, both in good and in evil, and thus in an ultimate meaning to life (justification by faith).

Instead of a Postscript   41

Preface

"Posting theses" has been linked in the past, especially at the Reformation, with unhappy experiences for certain theologians in the Church. But the world is different now, and so is the Church. I hope, therefore, to fare better with these theses.

Contrary to all pessimistic predictions, interest in what being a Christian means, in the distinctive Christian reality, has greatly increased. This is not merely a new, fashionable trend but the expression of a need—very understandable and justified, particularly today—for basic orientation, reliable exemplary values, ultimate and primary standards: in a word, for a meaning to man's life in the face of a constantly changing world and society. At a time when intellectual trends, ideologies, and often also theologies are quickly superseded, there is a need to concentrate on what is essential, decisive for the Christian cause.

The book *On Being a Christian* was and is meant to help satisfy this need. The success of the original version of the book—which is no lightweight—came as a surprise even to its author and shows how well his intentions were understood: an amazingly large measure of approval in Catholic, Protestant, and Free Church circles and even among those outside any church; on the part of people of the most diverse age groups, callings, educational levels, with very different mentalities.

The work has been criticized, as could be expected, from two sides: from the theological left and the theological right, working as so often in close harmony. On the left some would have welcomed it if a left-wing socialist ideology—for which even social democracy is too far to the right—had been made the criterion of what is Christian: Jesus of Nazareth a social revolutionary, his gospel the program of the revolution. On the right, not for the first time, a small, concerted action is in progress: As if by agreement, dogmatists present themselves as keepers of the Holy Grail of lofty dogmas which even they can scarcely make intelligible to modern man. But they have nothing to say about the many other things in this book which are perhaps more essential for becoming a Christian and which countless people will find more important for their lives as Christians.

One misunderstanding however must be avoided. If we dissociate ourselves from the demythologizers on the left and the mythologizers on the right, this does not mean that we stand for an "ideology of the center": neutralizing, minimizing, harmonizing. In regard to both theological and social questions we are upholding here a "radical" approach, understood in the light of the Jesus Christ of the New Testament, which gets at the roots (*radices*) of individual and social conflicts more effectively than the ideologized left or right radicalisms (which must certainly be distinguished from a genuine radicalness). In this sense it is a question of a "radical mean," which is anything but a detached "aloofness."

These twenty theses represent a summary of what I consider important for being a Christian at the present time. From my point of view, they sum up twenty years of theological research which went into the making of my book *On Being a Christian*. They can, however, also provide a first, concentrated survey for someone who wants to know what being a Christian means today. The exposition of the theses is neither a complete catechism nor a textbook of dogmatics; nevertheless, it represents in content and form an attempt at an up-to-date summary of the Christian faith. It may be helpful to those who are asking, not merely for a better Christian teaching, but particularly for a better Christian existence: for a Christianity with a more human face.

HANS KÜNG

Tübingen, July 1975

A. Who is a Christian?

---

1. No one is a Christian simply because he or she tries to live in a human or in a social or even in a religious way. That person alone is a Christian who tries to live his or her human, social, and religious life in the light of Jesus Christ.

---

a. What does being **human** mean? It means being truly human, truly man: striving for a full individual human existence.

But: this is possible even for the secular humanist, for the classical scholar of the type of a Humboldt or Gilbert Murray or the existentialist in the tradition of Heidegger or Sartre, or even the positivist with an outlook determined by the natural sciences or by a critical rationalism.

We should admit without more ado:

They can all be genuine humanists, really living in a human way. But they are not necessarily Christians on that account.

b. What does being **social** mean? It means being related to society: being oriented to the needs and hopes of our fellow men, of the other human groups, of society as a whole, and being actively committed to social justice.

But: this is possible even for someone who is socially committed in a secular sense; it is possible for both the liberal social reformer and equally the Marxist social revolutionary; it is possible also for a Spanish social-fascist, a South American socialist, or even a representative of the European and American New Left.

It cannot be disputed:

All these can uphold justified and urgent social demands. But they are not necessarily Christians on that account.

c. What does being **religious** mean? It means being bound back (*re-ligari*) or having regard (*re-legere*) to an absolute reality: living within the horizon of an absolute ground of being, oriented to something that involves me unconditionally.

But: this is possible even for a Buddhist or Hindu, a Muslim or Jew; it is possible for a devout pantheist or a skeptical deist, a spiritualistic mysticist, a follower of some sort of transcendental meditation (Yoga or Zen), or even merely the average man with religious feelings who seeks to justify his action before an authority binding on his conscience.

We should never have disputed it:

They can all be truly religious. But they are not necessarily Christians on that account.

What then is the distinctive Christian reality? What makes the Christian a Christian? In a word, the fact that he tries to live his human, social, and religious life in the light of Jesus Christ. He tries: no more and no less.

---

2. The distinctive Christian reality is Jesus Christ himself.

---

a. Against all often well-meant stretching, blending, misinterpreting and confusing of the meaning of what is Christian, things must be called by their true names, concepts taken at their face value. For the Christianity of Christians must remain Christian. But it remains Christian only if it remains explicitly **linked to the one Christ.** And he is not any sort of principle or an intentionality, not an attitude or an evolutionary goal. He is a quite definite, unmistakable, irreplaceable person with a quite definite name. In the light of this very name Christianity cannot be reduced or "elevated" to a nameless (anonymous) Christianity. The distinctive Christian reality is Christ himself.

b. Such a doctrinal formula is **not an empty formula.** Why?
* It refers to a very concrete historical person: Jesus of Nazareth.
* It has behind it therefore the Christian beginnings and also the whole great Christian tradition: That is Christian which has to do with this Christ.
* It offers a clear orientation for both present and future.
* It is helpful therefore to Christians and yet wins also the approval of non-Christians: since their convictions are respected and their values expressly affirmed, without being appropriated by dogmatic sleight of hand for Christianity and Church, as when they are told: "You are really Christians, at any rate anonymous Christians already."

Since in this way the concepts of what is Christian are not diluted or arbitrarily stretched but are precisely grasped and taken at their face value, two things are simultaneously possible:

All unchristian confusion can be avoided (greatest possible *unambiguity*) and at the same time open-mindedness for all that is non-Christian can be maintained (greatest possible *tolerance*).

c. According to this criterion, Christianity does not mean an exclusivism of salvation, but that **uniqueness** which is founded in Jesus Christ. In regard to the **world religions** this means:
* *not* the absolutist *domination of one religion,* claiming an exclusive mission and despising freedom;
* *not* the syncretist *mingling of all religions,* however much they contradict one another, harmonizing and reducing and thus suppressing the truth;
* *but* independent, unselfish Christian *service to men in the religions,* destroying nothing of value in the religions, but not incorporating uncritically anything worthless: In discriminating recognition and rejection, Christianity should act among the world religions as *critical catalyst and crystallization point* of their religious, moral, meditative, ascetic, aesthetic values.

In this orientation even today the Church can and should *proclaim Jesus Christ to all men,* in order precisely in this way to make possible a genuine Indian, Chinese, Japanese, Indonesian, Arab, African Christianity: an *oikoumene,* no longer in the narrow denominational-ecclesiastical sense but in a universal Christian sense.

3. **Being a Christian means: By following Jesus Christ, the human being in the world of today can truly humanly love, act, suffer, and die, in happiness and unhappiness, life and death, sustained by God and helpful to men.**

a. *Why should one be a Christian?* The answer, quite directly is: **In order to be truly human.** What does this mean?
Being Christian cannot mean ceasing to be human. But neither can being human mean ceasing to be Christian. Being Christian is not an addition to being human: There is not a Christian level above or below the human. The Christian should not be a split personality.

b. The Christian element therefore is neither a superstructure nor a substructure of the human, but—preserving, canceling and surpassing—a **transfiguration or "sublation"** [Aufhebung] **of the human,** of the other humanisms:
• They are *affirmed* to the extent that they affirm the human reality;
• they are *rejected* to the extent that they reject the Christian reality, Christ himself;
• they are *surpassed,* transcended, to the extent that being Christian can fully incorporate the human, all too human, even in all its *negativity.*

c. This means: Christians are no less humanists than all other humanists. But they see the human, the truly human, the humane; they see man and his God; see humanity, freedom, justice, life, love, peace, meaning: All these they see in the light of this Jesus who for them is **the concrete criterion, the Christ.** In his light they think they cannot support just any kind of humanism which simply affirms all that is true, good, beautiful and human. But they can support a truly **radical humanism** which is able to integrate and control what is untrue, not good, unlovely, inhuman: not only everything positive, but also—and here we discern what a humanism has to offer—everything negative, even suffering, sin, futility, death.

d. *Therefore:* By following this Jesus, even in the world of today, man is able not only to *act* but also to *suffer,* not only to *live* but also to *die,* in a truly human way. And even when "pure reason" breaks down, even in pointless misery and sin, he perceives a meaning: for he knows that here too, in both positive and negative experience, *he is sustained by God.* Thus faith in Jesus the Christ gives peace with God and with oneself but does not play down the problems of the world and society. It makes man truly human, because truly one with other men, *helpful to human beings:* unreservedly open (in serving, renouncing, pardoning) for the other person, the one who needs him here and now, his "neighbor."

B. Who is Christ?

> 4. The Christ is no other than the historical Jesus of Nazareth. Neither priest nor political revolutionary, neither ascetic monk nor devout moralist, he is provocative on all sides.

a. **Not a man of the priestly establishment:** There was a religio-political establishment in Jerusalem (Sadducees), and many later saw Jesus as a representative of the religio-ecclesiastical establishment.
Yet: Jesus was not a priest. He was a "layman"—oddly enough, not married—and ringleader of a lay movement. Neither was he a theologian: He produced no grandiose theories or systems. He preached the early advent of the kingdom of God, in an unscholarly way, in the simplest words, with comparisons, stories, parables.

b. **Not a political revolutionary:** There was a revolutionary party at that time (Zealots), and many—for instance, in South America—see Jesus in this light.
Yet: He was not in any case a political or a social revolutionary. If he had only carried out an agricultural reform or—as happened in the Jerusalem revolution after his death—had set on fire the bonds in the Jerusalem archives and organized a revolt against the Roman occupying power, he would have been forgotten long ago. But he proclaimed nonviolence and love of enemies.

c. **Not an ascetic monk:** In Palestine, in Jesus' own time, there existed a well-organized monasticism (Essenes, Qumran), and monks at all times have gladly invoked him as an example for their way of life.
Yet: Jesus did not in any way withdraw from the world, he did not

cut himself off from it, nor did he send anyone who wanted to be perfect to the great monastery of Qumran on the Dead Sea which has been rediscovered in recent times. He never founded an order with its rule, vows, ascetic precepts, special clothing, and traditions.

d. **Not a devout moralist:** There existed at that time a movement for moral rearmament: the Pharisees. And later people often regarded him as a "new lawgiver."
Yet: Jesus did not teach any "new law" or any technique of piety, nor had he any taste for moral or still less legal casuistry; he was not interested in questions of legal interpretation. He proclaimed a new freedom from legalism: love without limits.

Therefore: It shows considerable understanding of Jesus if we do not attempt to integrate him within the quadrilateral of establishment and revolution, emigration and compromise: He fits no formula. He is provocative, but both to right and to left: apparently closer than the priests to God. At the same time freer than the ascetics in regard to the world. More moral than the moralists. And more revolutionary than the revolutionaries.
Why could he not be integrated? This is connected with the question of what he wanted. What did he in fact want?

---

5. **Jesus did not proclaim any theological theory or any new law, nor did he proclaim himself. He proclaimed the kingdom of God: God's cause (= God's will), which will prevail and which is identical with man's cause (= man's well-being).**

The person of Jesus is subordinated to his cause. But Jesus' cause is God's cause: the kingdom of God which is coming soon.

a. **God's kingdom:** Jesus' message was never as complicated as our catechisms and certainly far less complicated than our theological textbooks. He proclaimed in metaphors and parables the coming kingdom of God: that *God's cause* will prevail, that the future belongs to God. That is:

• It is not merely God's continuing rule, existing from the dawn of creation, as understood by the religious leaders in Jerusalem, but the future eschatological kingdom of God.

• It is not the religio-political theocracy or democracy which the Zealot revolutionaries wanted to set up by force, but the direct, unrestricted rule of God himself over the world, to be awaited without recourse to violence.

• It is not the avenging judgment in favor of an elite of the perfect, as understood by the Essenes and the Qumran monks, but the glad tidings of God's infinite goodness and unconditional grace, particularly for the abandoned and destitute.

• It is not a kingdom to be constructed by men through an exact fulfillment of the law and better morals in the sense understood by the Pharisees, but the kingdom of the consummation to be created by God's free act.

b. Tension between present and future:

(1) The *present* directs man to *God's absolute future.* Our present time must not be made absolute at the expense of the future. The whole future of God's kingdom must not be frittered away in our preoccupation with the present. The present with its poverty and guilt is and remains too sad and too discordant to be already the kingdom of God. This world and society are too imperfect and inhuman to be already the perfect and definitive state of things. God's kingdom does not remain at its dawn but must finally break through. What began with Jesus must also be finished with Jesus. The immediate expectation was not fulfilled. But this is no reason for excluding all expectation.

(2) The *absolute future* throws man back on the *present.* The future cannot be isolated at the expense of the present. The kingdom of God cannot be merely a consoling promise for the future, the satisfaction of pious curiosity about the future, the projection of unfulfilled promises and fears (as Feuerbach, Marx, and Freud thought). It is precisely in the light of the future that man ought to be initiated into the present. It is by hope itself that the present world and society are to be not only interpreted but changed. Jesus did not

want to provide information about the end of time but to issue a call for the present in view of the approaching end.

c. **God's cause = man's cause.** In view of the coming kingdom Jesus preaches *a supreme norm* for man's action. It is not any sort of law or dogma, not a canon or a legal clause.

For him the supreme norm is the *will of God*. His will be done. This sounds very pious. But what is this will of God?

God's will is not simply identical with a particular law, a dogma, or a rule. From all that Jesus says and does, it is clear that God's will is nothing other than *man's total well-being*. The Beatitudes of the Sermon on the Mount and not least the healing stories (expulsions of demons) bring out the fact that it is a question not only of the salvation of souls but of the salvation of the whole man at the present time and in the future. What kind of well-being and what individual person is meant here cannot be precisely established in principle or in a legal sense. In constantly varying situations it is always a question of the very definite well-being of anyone who needs me here and now, my neighbor at any particular moment. What does this mean in the concrete according to Jesus?

---

6. **For the sake of men's well-being Jesus effectively relativized sacred institutions, law, and cult.**

God wills men's well-being:

a. *Therefore* Jesus, who is generally completely faithful to the law, does not hesitate in a particular case to **act in a manner contrary to law.**
• He has no interest in ritual correctitude: Only purity before God bestows purity of heart.
• He does not cultivate any asceticism of fasting: He allows people to call him a glutton and a drunkard.
• He is not scrupulous about Sabbath observance: Man is the measure of the Sabbath and the law.

b. *Therefore* he effectively **relativizes** in a scandalous way sacred **traditions and institutions:**
- He relativizes the law, the whole religio-social system: for the commandments exist for man's sake. The law is not simply abolished or annulled. But man replaces a legal system which has been made absolute; humanity replaces legalism and dogmatism. All norms and institutions, clauses and dogmas are judged by the criterion of whether they exist for man or not.
- He relativizes the temple and its cult: for reconciliations and everyday service to men come before the liturgy. The liturgy is not simply abolished or annulled. But man replaces a liturgy which has been made absolute. Humanity replaces formalism and ritualism. All rites and customs, practices and ceremonies are judged by the criterion of whether they exist for man or not.

c. *Therefore* he stood for the **love** which permits a person to be both devout and reasonable and which is proved by the very fact that it excludes no one, not **even opponents,** but is prepared to go to the point of
- service regardless of rank,
- renunciation without anything in return,
- forgiveness without limits.
That is: changing society by radically changing the individual.

d. *Therefore* to the scandal of the devout, he **identifies** himself with **all the poor,** the wretched, the "poor devils":
the heretics and schismatics (Samaritans), the immoral (prostitutes and adulterers), the politically compromised (tax collectors and collaborators), those outside and neglected by society (lepers, sick, destitute), the weak (women and children), on the whole with the common people (who do not know what is really involved).

e. *Therefore,* instead of the legal penalty, he ventures to proclaim God's **forgiveness**—completely gratis—and even personally to award forgiveness, thus making possible conversion and forgiveness for our fellow men.

7. Jesus thus asserted a claim to be advocate of God and men. He provoked a final decision: not for a particular title, a dogma, or law but for his good news. But in this way, too, the question of his person was indirectly raised: heretical teacher, false prophet, blasphemer, seducer of the people—or what?

a. **Claim:** As an obvious outsider Jesus became involved in a critically dangerous social *conflict:* in opposition to the prevailing conditions and in opposition to the people who opposed them.

This was an enormous claim, but there was apparently *little behind it:* lowly origin, no support from his family, without special education. He had no money, held no office, had received no honors, had no retinue; he was not backed by any party nor authorized by any tradition. How could a man without power claim such *authority?* Who in fact was for him?

But: while his teaching and his whole conduct exposed him to fatal attacks, he found also spontaneous trust and love.

In a word: He represented the parting of the ways.

b. **Decision:** Jesus had become a public person. Confronted by him, the people and particularly the hierarchy found themselves *faced with an inescapable final decision:* but not a Yes or No to a particular title, to a particular dignity, a particular office, or even to a particular dogma, rite, or law.

His message and community raised the question of the *aim and purpose* to which a man will *ultimately* direct his life. Jesus demanded a final decision for God's cause and man's. In this "cause" he is completely absorbed, without demanding anything for his own person, without making his own "role" or dignity the theme of his message.

c. **Cause and person:** The great question about his person was raised only indirectly and the mystery deepened as a result of his avoidance of any titles.

Jesus, for whom theory and practice inextricably coincided, presented an *unparalleled challenge* to the whole religious-social system (law) and its representatives (hierarchy). What really is his authority for doing this? This was the question asked by friends and foes. Here is someone who proclaims, instead of absolute fulfillment of the law, a remarkable freedom for God and man. Does he not make himself greater than Moses (law), greater than Solomon (temple), greater than Jonah (prophet)? Are not people bound to take offense?

- Is a teacher of the law who sets himself up against Moses not a *heretical teacher?*
- Is a prophet who does not belong to the succession from Moses not a *pseudo prophet?*
- Is someone claiming to be above Moses and the prophets, who even assumes the function of a final judge in regard to sin, thus intruding in a sphere that belongs to God alone, not—this must be clearly stated—a *blasphemer?*
- Is he not anything but the innocent victim of a stubborn people and in fact a fanatic and heretic, as such a supremely dangerous demagogue, very seriously threatening the position of the hierarchy, disturbing the existing order, stirring up unrest, *seducing the people?* At this point a still more serious question arises: Is he not in fact preaching a different God?

---

8. **In the last resort the conflict centers on God. Jesus does not invoke a new God. He invokes the God of Israel— understood in a new way, as Father of the abandoned, whom he addresses quite personally as his Father.**

---

a. **Father of the abandoned:** It is the *God of Israel,* the God of the Fathers, whom Jesus invokes for all his talk and action. But, if he were right, what would this God be like? Jesus' whole proclamation and action raises in a way that is finally inescapable the question of

God: what he is like and what he is not like, what he does and what
he does not do. In the last resort the whole conflict centers on the
one true God himself.

Yet it is a *very different God* and Father whom Jesus invokes to justify his scandalous talk and conduct: a curious, even dangerous, a really impossible God. Or can we really assume

• that God himself justifies infringements of the law?

• that God himself ruthlessly sets himself above the righteousness of
  the law and has a "higher righteousness" proclaimed?

• that he himself therefore permits the existing legal order and thus
  the whole social system, and even the temple and divine worship,
  to be called in question?

• that God himself makes man the measure of his commandments;
  that through forgiving, serving, renouncing, through love, he can-
  cels the natural frontiers between comrades and noncomrades,
  strangers and neighbors, friends and foes, good and bad, and thus
  places himself on the side of the weak, sick, poor, underprivileged,
  oppressed, and even of the irreligious, immoral, and godless?

This would certainly be a new God: a God who has set himself free
from his own law, a God not of the devout observers of the law but
of the lawbreakers—in fact, not a God of God-fearers, but a God of
the godless. This would be a truly unparalleled revolution in the understanding of God.

b. **The Father of Jesus:** Jesus' whole message of God's kingdom and
will is oriented to God as "Father." This Father he addresses with
natural directness, singular immediacy, and scandalous familiarity as
his Father.

The peculiarly new proclaiming and addressing of God as Father
threw its light on the person who proclaimed and addressed him in
this strangely new way. And, as it was impossible even then to speak
of Jesus without speaking of this God and Father, so it was difficult
subsequently to speak of this God and Father without speaking of
Jesus. When it was a question of the *one true God,* the decision of
faith was centered not on particular names and titles but on this
Jesus. The way in which someone came to terms with Jesus decided
how he stood with God, what he made of God, what God he had.
Jesus spoke and acted in the name and in the power of the one God
of Israel. And for this God finally he let himself be slain.

9. Jesus' violent end was the logical consequence of this approach of his to God and man. His violent passion was the reaction of the guardians of the law, justice, and morality to his nonviolent action: the crucifixion becomes the fulfillment of the curse of the law; Jesus becomes the representative of lawbreakers, of sinners. He dies forsaken by both men and God.

a. **Death as consequence:** Jesus did not merely passively suffer death but actively provoked it.
• Only his proclamation explains his condemnation.
• Only his action explains his suffering.
• Only the life and work as a whole make clear what distinguishes the cross of this one person from the many crosses of world history.

b. **The curse of the law:** For that time the death of Jesus meant that the law had conquered. Put in question radically by Jesus, it had retaliated and killed him. Its curse had struck him. Being crucified, Jesus was cursed by God.
Thus his claim is refuted, his authority gone, his way proved to be false: the heretical teacher, pseudo prophet, seducer of the people, blasphemer is condemned. The law has triumphed over this "gospel": there is nothing in this "higher righteousness" based on a faith opposed to the righteousness of the law which is based on good works.

c. **Representative of sinners:** Thus Jesus appears as sin personified. He is literally the representative of all lawbreakers and outlaws, whom he has defended and who really deserve the same fate as he: the representative of sinners in the worst sense of the word.

d. **God-forsakenness:** Here however lies the singularity of this death. Jesus died not merely forsaken by men but absolutely forsaken by God. The *unique communion with God* which he had seemed to enjoy only *made his forsakenness more unique.* This God and Father with whom he had completely identified himself to the very end did not at the end identify himself with the sufferer.

And so everything seemed as if it had never been: in vain. He who had announced the closeness and the advent of God, his Father, publicly before the whole world, dies completely forsaken by God and is thus publicly demonstrated as *godless* before the whole world: someone judged by God himself, disposed of once and for all.

And since the *cause* for which he had lived and fought was so closely linked with his *person,* so that cause fell with his person. There was no cause independent of himself. How could anyone have believed his word after he had been silenced and died in this outrageous way?

The end of everything? Or was Jesus' death perhaps not the end of everything? Here particularly we must exercise great caution.

---

10. **Jesus' death, however, was not the end of everything. The faith of his community is: The Crucified is living forever with God, as our hope. Resurrection does not mean either a return to life in space and time or a continuation of life in space and time but the assumption into that incomprehensible and comprehensive last and first reality which we call God.**

---

a. **The Crucified is living:** Was his death the end of everything? Evidently not. There is no doubt among historians about the fact that the movement emanating from Jesus properly began only after his death.

What was the reason for it?

When we look through the different conflicting traditions and legendary elaborations of the Easter stories, there remains the *unanimous testimony of the first believers,* who regarded their faith as based on something that really happened to them: The Crucified is living forever with God, as hope for us. The men of the New Testament are sustained, impelled, by the certainty that the man who was killed did not remain dead but is alive and that anyone who clings to him in trust and faith will likewise live. The new, eternal life of the One is a real hope for all.

b. What does "living" mean here?

* *Not a return* to this life in space and time: Death is not canceled (no revival of a corpse) but definitively conquered (entry into a wholly different, imperishable, eternal, "heavenly" life).
* *Not a continuation* of this life in space and time: Even to speak of life "after" death is misleading; eternity is not characterized by "before" and "after." It means a new life which escapes the dimensions of space and time, a life within God's invisible, imperishable, incomprehensible domain ("heaven").
* *Resurrection means positively:* Jesus did not die into nothingness, but in death and out of death was assumed into that incomprehensible and comprehensive last and first reality, by that most real reality which we designate with the name of God. When man reaches his eschaton, the absolutely final point in his life, what awaits him there? Not nothing, but that All which is God. The believer knows that death is transition to God, retreat into God's hiddenness, into that domain which surpasses all imagination, which no human eye has ever seen, eluding our grasp, comprehension, reflection, or imagination.

---

11. **The resurrection faith, therefore, is not an appendage but a radicalizing of faith in God: of faith in God the Creator.**

---

a. **Radicalizing of faith in God:** The resurrection faith is not an appendage to faith in God: It is a faith in God which does not stop halfway but follows the road consistently to the end. It is a faith in which man, without strictly rational proof but certainly with completely reasonable trust, relies on the fact that the God of the beginning is also the God of the end, that as he is the Creator of the world and man, so too he is their Completer.

b. **Radicalizing of faith in God the Creator:** The resurrection faith then is not to be interpreted merely as existential interiorization or social change but as a radicalizing of faith in God the Creator.

Resurrection means the real conquest of death by God the Creator, to whom faith entrusts everything, even the ultimate, even the conquest of death. The end which is a new beginning.

Anyone who begins his creed with faith in "God the almighty Creator" may be content also to end it with faith in "eternal life." Since God is the Alpha, he is also the Omega. Only an atheist can really maintain that death is the end of *everything*.

c. **From proclaimer to proclaimed:** According to the unanimous New Testament accounts, Jesus of Nazareth, himself, perceived and recognized as living, is the reason why his cause continued. Here lies the answer to the enigma of the emergence of Christianity, the reason

• why after his death the Jesus-movement with its immense consequences came into existence, after Jesus' failure a new beginning, after the flight of the disciples a community of believers which is called Church;

• why this heretical teacher, false prophet, seducer of the people, and blasphemer, discredited and judged by God, was proclaimed with quite frantic boldness as Messiah of God, Christ, as the Lord, Savior, and Son of God;

• why the shameful gallows could be understood as a sign of victory;

• why the first witnesses, sustained in the last resort by a confidence without fear of contempt, persecution, and death, spread such scandalous news of an executed man as glad tidings (gospel— *euangelion*) among men;

• why therefore Jesus was not only venerated, studied, and followed as founder and teacher but perceived as actively present in "spirit";

• why the mystery of God was seen to be linked with his turbulent, enigmatic history and thus Jesus himself was made the real content of their proclamation;

• why he became the summary of the message of God's kingdom, why the person who called for faith became the content of faith, why the proclaiming Jesus became the Jesus proclaimed.

> 12. Without faith in the risen Christ, faith in the crucified Jesus lacks confirmation and authorization. Without faith in the cross, faith in the risen Christ lacks its distinctive character and decisiveness. The ultimate distinctive feature of Christianity is Jesus Christ as the Crucified.

a. What then is the ultimate distinctive feature?

As already established in a first outline of the problem, the distinguishing feature of Christianity as opposed to the ancient world religions and modern humanisms is this *Christ himself.*

But what protects us against any confusion of this Christ with other religious or political messiahs and Christ-figures?

The ultimate distinctive feature of Christianity—as more closely defined in Thesis 4—is the Christ, who is identical with the real, historical Jesus of Nazareth: It is therefore in the concrete this Christ *Jesus.*

But what protects us against any confusion of this historical Christ Jesus with false Jesus-images?

The *ultimate* distinctive feature of Christianity—the definitive answer can now be given—is quite literally according to Paul "this Jesus Christ, Jesus Christ *crucified*" (1 Cor. 2:2).

b. Cross and resurrection:

It is not indeed as risen, exalted, living, divine but as crucified that this Jesus Christ is distinguished unmistakably from the many risen, exalted, living gods and deified founders of religions, from the Caesars, geniuses, and heroes of world history.

The *cross* then is not only example and model but ground, strength, and norm of the Christian faith: the *great distinctive reality* which radically distinguishes this faith and its Lord in the world market from the religious and irreligious ideologies, from other competing religions and utopias and their lords, and at the same time plunges its roots into the reality of concrete life with its conflicts: *"Jesus is Lord"*—this is the oldest and most concise Christian creed.

The cross then separates the Christian faith from unbelief and superstition. The cross certainly in the light of the resurrection, but also the resurrection in the shadow of the cross.

---

13. The emergence of the Church can be explained only in the light of faith in Jesus raised to life: the Church of Jesus Christ as the community of those who have committed themselves to the cause of Jesus Christ and bear witness to it as hope for all men.

---

a. **Origin:** Jesus did not found a church during his lifetime. Neither the supporters of Jesus who are prepared simply to repent nor the disciples called in a special way to follow him nor the twelve were set apart from Israel by Jesus as a "new people of God" or as a "church" and contrasted with the ancient people of God. It is only *after Jesus' death* and raising to life that primitive Christendom speaks of a "church": "Church" in the sense of a special community distinct from Israel is quite clearly a post-Easter factor. Its basis at first is not a cult of its own, a constitution of its own, an organization of its own with special ministries, but simply and solely the profession of faith in this Jesus as the Christ. It is the "Church of Jesus Christ."

b. **Task:** The Church's one task is to serve the cause of Jesus Christ in every sense, not to obstruct it, therefore, but to realize it for its own sake in the spirit of Jesus Christ and give effect to it in modern society as hope for all men. Among the *basic functions* of this service are: the proclamation of the Christian message, baptism in the name of Jesus, the thanksgiving meal (eucharist) in memory of him, assurance of forgiveness of sins and daily service to one's fellow man and to society.

c. **Local and universal Church:** Church (= ekklesia = assembly = congregation) is the community of those who believe in Jesus Christ, and it means both local Church and universal Church. The *local Church* is not merely a "section" or a "province" of the universal Church. On the other hand, the *universal Church* is not merely an "accumulation" or "association" of local Churches. But every local Church—however small, insignificant, modest, poor—realizes, manifests, represents fully the whole Church of Jesus Christ (biblical images for both include people of God, body of Christ, temple of the Holy Spirit).

d. **Structure:** On the basis of a liberty, equality and fraternity founded in the Christian message, there are in the Church countless *differences,* not only of persons but also of functions, and therefore, too, a multiple, functionally defined super- and subordination. In the Church, too, therefore there is human authority. But it is legitimate only when it is based on service and not on naked or concealed power, on old or new privileges. Instead of speaking of "office" in the Church, it would be better to adopt the more precise biblical usage and to talk of "service" or "ministry": of very many and very varied *"ministries"* or *"charisms"* (special vocations).

Among the permanent public ministries the *ministry of leadership or presidency,* which continues the ministry of the apostles in founding and leading churches, occupies a special place. Its function is public provision for the common cause at the local, regional, or universal level: in virtue of a special vocation to lead the Christian community continuously in the spirit of Jesus Christ. That is, to stimulate, co-or-dinate, and integrate the community, to represent it outside and also to its own members—all this through the proclamation of the word together with the celebration of the sacraments and active involve-ment in congregation and society.

e. **Apostolic succession:** Apostolic succession, agreement with the apostolic testimony (transmitted to us in the New Testament) and the continual implementation of the apostolic ministry (missionary advance into the world and building up of the congregation), is quite *universally* required of the whole Church and each individual Chris-tian. But inasmuch as the ministries of leadership in particular (bishops and pastors) carry on in a special way the apostolic mis-sion of founding and leading churches, we can rightly speak of a *spe-cial* apostolic succession in a functional sense on the part of these ministries of leadership. *Entry* into this apostolic succession of the ministries of leadership can of course come about in *various* ways. Normally it takes the form of a calling by the church leaders (with the participation of the congregation). But in principle, according to the New Testament, anyone can become a church leader as a result of a calling by other members of the congregation or in virtue of the spontaneous appearance of a charism for leading or founding a church. To that extent the ministries of the Protestant churches can also claim full validity. In the light of the New Testament, a number of church constitutions are legitimate, even if they are not all equally appropriate or practicable. We must strive to remove the divisions between the churches with their different constitutions.

---

14. **The essential distinction between "Catholic" and "Protestant" today no longer lies in particular doctrinal differences but in the diversity of basic attitudes which have developed since the Reformation but which can now be overcome in their one-sidedness and integrated into a true ecumenicity.**

---

a. The particular **traditional doctrinal differences** relate to scripture and tradition, sin and grace, faith and works, eucharist and priesthood, Church and papacy. On all these issues a theoretical agreement is at least possible or has already been attained. All that is required is for church leaders to draw the theological conclusions and put them into practice.

b. The essential distinction lies in **traditional basic attitudes** built up from the Reformation period:
• *Catholic* as a basic attitude means that special importance is attached to the "catholic"—that is, to the *entire,* universal, all-encompassing, total—Church. In the concrete, importance is attached to the *continuity* in time of faith and the community of faith enduring in all disruptions (tradition) and to the *universality* in space of faith and the community of faith embracing all groups (against "Protestant" radicalism and particularism, which are not to be confused with evangelical radicality and congregational attachment).
• *Protestant* as a basic attitude means that in all traditions, doctrines,

and practices of the Church, special importance is attached to constant critical recourse to the *gospel* (scripture) and to constant practical *reform* according to the norm of the gospel (against "Catholic" traditionalism and syncretism, which are not to be confused with Catholic tradition and breadth of vision).

c. Yet, correctly understood, Catholic and Protestant basic attitudes *are by no means mutually exclusive.* Today even the "born" Catholic can be truly Protestant in his outlook and even the "born" Protestant truly Catholic, so that even now in the whole world there are innumerable Christians who—despite the obstructions of the Church's machinery—do in fact live out an "evangelical Catholicity" centered on the gospel or a "Catholic evangelicity" maintaining a Catholic breadth of vision: In a word, they realize a genuine *ecumenicity.* In this way a Christian today can be a Christian in the full sense without denying his own denominational past but also without obstructing a better ecumenical future. Being truly a Christian today means being an ecumenical Christian.

---

15. **The ecumenical basis of all Christian churches is the biblical profession of faith in Jesus as the Christ, as the criterion for man's relations with God and with his fellow men. This profession of faith must be freshly translated for each new age.**

---

a. In the history of faith new expressions have constantly been found for the fact that *God himself* in the work and person of Jesus encounters man, manifests himself—admittedly not in a way perceptible to the neutral observer, but certainly for the person who believes and commits himself trustfully to Jesus. Thus the true man, Jesus of Nazareth, for the Church's faith is **the real revelation of the one true God.**

b. Despite all continuity of faith, in the course of the history of the Church, this acknowledgment of Jesus Christ has been **differently interpreted** in theological terms in the light of the times, and it has therefore to be constantly translated afresh for the present while keeping in mind what has come into existence historically (tradition): not another gospel, but the same ancient gospel freshly discovered for today.

c. That **God and man are truly involved** in the story of Jesus Christ is something to be steadfastly upheld by faith even today. It must also—and particularly—be upheld when divine sonship, pre-existence, creation-mediatorship, incarnation are to be freshly interpreted for the present time. Nor, in the light of the New Testament, can any interpretation of the story of Jesus Christ be justified today in which Jesus Christ is "only God": a God moving about on earth, relieved of human defects and weaknesses. But neither must he be seen as "only man": only a preacher, prophet, or sage, a symbol or cipher for universally human basic experiences.

d. Perhaps after these negative demarcations, based on the New Testament, we may attempt without any claim to infallibility an up-to-date positive interpretation of the **classical formula** which has been binding since the fifth century: "true God and true man" (Council of Chalcedon, A.D. 451, following Nicaea, A.D. 325):

- **Truly God:** The whole point of what happened in and with Jesus of Nazareth depends on the fact that, for believers, *God himself* as man's friend was present, speaking, acting, definitively revealing himself *in Jesus,* who came among men as God's advocate and deputy, representative and delegate, and who, as the Crucified raised to life, was confirmed by God. All statements about divine sonship, pre-existence, creation-mediatorship, and incarnation— often clothed in the mythological or semimythological forms of the time—are meant in the last resort to do no more and no less than substantiate the *uniqueness, underivability and unsurpassability* of the *call, offer, and claim* made known in and with Jesus, ultimately not of human but of divine origin and therefore absolutely reliable, requiring men's unconditional involvement.
- **Truly man:** Against all tendencies to deify Jesus, it must constantly be stressed even today, without any minimizing, that he was *wholly and entirely man,* with all the consequences of this (capacity for

suffering, fear, loneliness, insecurity, temptations, doubts, possibility of error). He was not, however, a mere man but *true man*. In describing him as such, we insist on the truth which has to be made true, the unity of theory and practice, of acknowledging and following him, of faith and action. As true man, by his proclamation, behavior, and fate, he provided a *model of what it is to be human,* enabling each and every one who commits himself trustfully to it to discover and realize the meaning of being man and of his freedom in existing for his fellow men. As confirmed by God, he therefore represents the permanently reliable ultimate *standard of human existence.*

e. Nothing, therefore, is to be deducted from the truth taught by the ancient Christological councils, so far as this is really covered by the New Testament, even though it must constantly be taken out of the sociocultural Hellenistic context and transferred to the mental climate of our own time. The important thing is not the consistency of terminology and conceptuality but the consistency of the main intentions and essential contents.

According to the New Testament, the final test of being a Christian is not assent to this or that dogma—however sublime—about Christ, nor agreement with a Christology or theory of Christ, but the acceptance of **faith in Christ** and the **following of Christ.**

C. Who Acts as a Christian?

16. The distinctive feature of Christian action, therefore, is the following of Christ. This Jesus Christ is in person the living, archetypal embodiment of his cause: embodiment of a new attitude to life and a new way of life. As a concrete, historical person, Jesus Christ possesses an impressiveness, audibility, and realizability which is missing in an eternal idea, an abstract principle, a universal norm, a conceptual system.

a. **Following:** This is what distinguishes Christians from disciples and supporters of other great men, in the sense that Christians are ultimately dependent on this person, not only on his teaching but also on his life, death, and new life. No Marxist or Freudian would want to claim this for his teacher. Although Marx and Freud personally composed their works, these can be studied and followed without any special commitment to their authors. Their works, their doctrines, are separable in principle from their persons.

We understand the gospel, however, the "teaching" (message) itself of Jesus in its essential meaning, only in the light of his life, death, and new life. In the New Testament as a whole his "teaching" is *inseparable from his person.* For Christians then Jesus is certainly a teacher but at the same time essentially more than a teacher: He is in person the living, archetypal embodiment of his cause.

"Following" then means committing myself to him and his way and *going my own way*—each has his own way—*in the light of his directions.* This possibility was seen from the very beginning as a great

opportunity: not a "must" but a "may," a true gift, true grace
which requires us only to grasp it in trust and faith and adapt our
lives according to it. The important thing is the new attitude to life
and the new way of life which it defines.

b. **Impressiveness:** A concrete person does not merely stimulate
thinking and critical-rational discourse, but also continually rouses
fantasy, imagination, and emotions, spontaneity, creativity, and inno-
vation: In a word, he appeals to man at every level. Only a living
figure and not a principle can *draw* people, can be "attractive" in the
most profound and comprehensive sense of the term: *Verba docent,
exempla trahunt.*

c. **Audibility:** A concrete, historical person has his unmistakable
proper name. And the name of Jesus can signify a power, a protection, a refuge, a claim. For this name is opposed to inhumanity, oppression, untruthfulness, and injustice and stands for humanity, freedom, justice, truth, and love. A concrete, historical person has words
and a voice. He can call and appeal. Only a living figure and not a
principle can make sweeping *demands:* Only such a figure can invite,
summon, challenge.

d. **Realizability:** A concrete, historical person is indisputably real,
even though this personality is open to different interpretations. With
the person of Jesus and his way we are dealing not with a pure possibility but with a possibility realized. Looking to him, man can know
that his way *is* to be followed and maintained. Here, then, there is no
question of simply imposing an imperative: You shall go on this
way, be justified, liberated. An indicative is presupposed: He went
by this way and—because of him—you *are* justified, liberated. Only
a living figure and not a principle can be *encouraging* in this comprehensive fashion. Only such a figure can stir people in this way to follow him, inspiring and strengthening their confidence that they too
can go by this way, dispelling doubts about their ability to do good
actions.

17. Jesus then means for modern man a basic model of a view of life and practice of life to be realized in many ways. Both positively and negatively he is in person invitation ("you may"), appeal ("you should"), challenge ("you can"), for the individual and society. He makes possible in the concrete a new basic orientation and basic attitude, new motivations, dispositions, projects, a new background of meaning and a new objective.

As the standard basic model of a view of life and practice of life, Jesus does not provide a scheme of life, a political system, or a social order in legal form but quite concretely inviting, binding, and challenging *examples, significant deeds, model cases, exemplary values, orientation standards.*
And by this very fact he impresses and influences, changes and transforms believers and thus human society. What Jesus quite concretely conveys and makes possible both to the individual and to the community may be described as follows:

a. **A new basic orientation and basic attitude:** a new attitude to life, to which Jesus summoned men and women and whose consequences he indicated. If an individual or a community have in mind this Jesus Christ as concrete example and living model for their relations with man, world, and God, they may and can live differently, more genuinely, more humanly. He makes possible an identity and inner coherence in life.

b. **New motivations:** new motives of action which can be discovered from Jesus' "theory" and "practice." In his light it is possible to answer the question why a person should act just in one way and not in another; why he should love and not hate; why—and even Freud had no answer to this—he should be honest, forbearing, and—wherever possible—kind, even when he loses by it and is made to suffer as a result of the unreliability and brutality of other people.

c. **New dispositions:** new consistent insights, tendencies, intentions, formed and maintained in the spirit of Jesus Christ. Here readiness to oblige is engendered, attitudes created, qualifications conveyed which can guide conduct not only for isolated and passing moments but permanently. Here we find dispositions of unpretentious commitment for one's fellow men, of identification with the handicapped, for the fight against unjust structures; dispositions of gratitude, freedom, magnanimity, unselfishness, joy, and also of forbearance, pardon, and service; dispositions which are proved also in borderline situations, in readiness for complete self-sacrifice, in renunciation even when it is not necessary, in a readiness to work for the greater cause.

d. **New projects:** new actions on a greater or smaller scale, which in the following of Jesus Christ begin at the very point where no one wants to help; not only universal programs to transform society but concrete signs, testimonies, evidence of humanity and the humanizing of both the individual and human society.

e. **A new background of meaning and a new objective:** in the ultimate reality, in the consummation of man and mankind in God's kingdom, which can sustain not only what is positive in human life but also what is negative. In the following of Jesus Christ the believer is given an ultimate meaning not only for man's life and action but also for his suffering and death, not only for mankind's success story but also for the story of its suffering.

---

18. **For the Church, too, Jesus must remain the authoritative standard in all things. The Church is credible only when it follows in his way as a provisional, serving, guilty, determined Church. At all times practical consequences must be drawn from this for constant internal church reform and for ecumenical understanding.**

The Church is not the kingdom of God, but it may and should be spokesman and witness of the kingdom of God. The Church is a *credible* witness only if it tells Jesus' message first of all not to others but to itself, and at the same time does not merely preach but also fulfills Jesus' requirements. Its whole credibility therefore depends on its *fidelity to Jesus and his cause.* In this sense none of the present-day churches—not even the Catholic Church—is automatically and in every respect identical with the Church of Jesus Christ. This identity exists only to the extent that a church keeps faith with Jesus and his cause. Then it goes on its way as a provisional, serving Church, aware of its guilt, but determined on its end.

a. **Provisional Church:** A community of faith which always remembers that it will find its end not in itself but in God's kingdom can hold out through all historical upheavals. It knows then that it has no need to construct a definitive system or to offer a lasting home; being provisional, it knows better than to be surprised when it is tempted by doubts, blocked by obstacles, burdened with problems.

b. **Serving Church:** If a community of faith remains aware of the fact that what is to come is not itself, but God's kingdom "in power and glory," if it finds its true greatness in its littleness, then it knows it is great precisely without display of power and application of force. It knows that its dignity is to be found only in unselfish service to society, to individuals and groups, and even to its opponents. It knows that nevertheless its existence is constantly ignored, neglected, and merely tolerated, deplored, reproached, or wished out of the way by society. But it knows too that God's power rules unassailably over all other powers and that it can itself have a saving effect on the nations and in men's hearts.

c. **Guilty Church:** If a community of faith with a history of fidelity and infidelity, of knowledge and error, takes seriously the fact that it is only in God's kingdom that good and bad, truth and error will be separated, then it will be awarded by grace that holiness which it cannot produce for itself. It knows then that it has no need to present a spectacle of higher morality to society, as if everything in it were ordered for the best. It knows that its faith is weak, its knowledge dim, its profession of faith halting, that there is not a single sin or failing of which it has not in one way or another been guilty, and, therefore, in all its dissociation from sin it has no reason to dissociate itself from sinners of any kind.

d. **Determined Church:** If a community of faith—despite all its failures—remains always intent on the kingdom coming through God's act and remembers for whom it was decided, it becomes truly free: free in following Christ for service to the world, free for service to men in which it serves God, and free for service to God in which it serves men. It becomes free even for the conquest of suffering, sin, and death, in the power of the cross of the living Jesus. It is free for the all-embracing love which even now does not merely interpret but transforms the broken world in virtue of unshakable hope in the coming kingdom of complete justice, of eternal life, of true freedom, of unlimited love, and of future peace: hope therefore of the removal of all estrangement and the final reconciliation of mankind with God.

e. **Practical suggestions:** Such a reflection on the gospel of Jesus Christ as center and foundation of the Church must lead at all times to practical consequences. Today especially in two respects:
(1) for increasing *ecumenical integration* of the different churches: through reform and reciprocal recognition of the ecclesial ministries; through a common liturgy of the word, open communion, and increasingly frequent common eucharistic celebrations; through common construction and common use of churches and other buildings; through a common fulfillment of service to society; through increasing integration of theological faculties and of religious instruction; through concrete plans for union worked out by the leaders of the churches at national and universal levels.
(2) for *internal church reform* even and particularly of the Catholic Church: in regard to the style of church leadership, election of bishops and popes, compulsory celibacy, coresponsibility of the laity, equal status of woman (ordination), freedom of conscience in questions of morality (birth control).

19. It is particularly in coping with the negative side of life that Christian faith and non-Christian humanisms have to face their acid text. For the Christian the only appropriate way to cope with the negative is in the light of the cross. Following the cross does not mean cultic adoration, mystical absorption, or ethical imitation. It means practice in a variety of ways in accordance with the cross of Jesus, in which a person freely perceives and attempts to follow his own way of life and suffering.

a. **Misunderstandings:** We do not want to waste time here on the countless crude distortions of the following of the cross, however serious their consequences may be both for the individual and for whole areas of the Church. How much dirty work has been done with the aid of the cross. But, for the sake of a genuine following of the cross, we must point out three of the more sublime misunderstandings of the message of the cross:

• Following the cross does *not* mean *cultic adoration:* The cross of Jesus cannot be confined within the systematic theology of sacrifice nor within the scheme of cultic practice. The very profaneness of the cross bars any cultic appropriation or liturgical glorification of the Crucified.

• Following the cross does *not* mean *mystical absorption:* It cannot mean convulsive, privatized sharing in suffering on the same plane, becoming united in prayer and meditation with Jesus' mental and physical pains. This would be a wrongly understood mysticism of the cross.

• Following the cross does *not* mean *ethical imitation* of Jesus' way of life. It does not mean producing a faithful copy of the model of his living, preaching, and dying; this would be impossible.

b. **Accord:** By the very fact of separating the cross from its copy, it is and remains a challenge, to accept one's own suffering, to go on *one's own way of life and suffering* in the midst of the risks of one's own situation and uncertain of the future. That is:

● not seeking, but bearing suffering;
● not only bearing, but fighting suffering;
● not only fighting, but utilizing suffering.

In a word, *freedom in suffering*. This means in the concrete:

Man's life in any sort of social or economic system is crisscrossed; it consists of events determined by the cross—by pain, care, suffering, and death. Only *in the light of the cross of Jesus* does man's crisscrossed existence acquire a *meaning*. Discipleship is always—sometimes in a hidden way, sometimes openly—a discipleship of suffering, a following of the cross. Does a man submit to this? It is under his cross that he comes nearest to Jesus, his crucified Lord. His own passion is set within the passion of Jesus Christ. And this very fact enables him in all suffering to enjoy an ultimate sovereign *superiority*. For no cross in the world can refute the offer of meaning issued on the cross of the One who was raised to life:

that even suffering, even extreme peril, futility, triviality, abandonment, loneliness and emptiness, are encompassed by a God who identifies himself with men;

that a way is thus opened to the believer, not indeed bypassing, but going right through suffering, so that his active indifference to suffering itself prepares him for the struggle against suffering and its causes, in the life of the individual and of society.

---

20. **Yet, despite all demands for action, looking to the crucified Jesus, the ultimately important thing for man will not be his achievements (justification by works), but his absolute trust in God, both in good and in evil, and thus in an ultimate meaning to life (justification by faith).**

---

a. **Justification by achievement:** In the modern efficiency-oriented society man experiences what Paul called the "curse of the law." Modern life constrains him to keep up his achievements, to continue to make progress, to be successful. He must constantly *justify his own existence:* no longer as formerly before the judgment seat of

God but before the forum of his milieu, before society, before himself. And it is only by achievement that he can justify himself in this efficiency-oriented society: Only by achievements is he something, does he keep his place in society, does he gain the esteem he needs.

But: with all his achievements, with all his activity, man does not by any means acquire being, identity, freedom, personality; he does not gain any self-assurance or discover the meaning of his existence. If someone only wants to reassure himself, to justify himself, life will elude him.

b. **What is not important:** There is also another way: Not simply to do nothing; not to refrain in principle from achievement; not to decry it in principle. But to know that the whole man is not absorbed in his calling and in his work, that achievements—good or bad—are important but not decisive. In a word: that in the last resort, in God's sight, *achievements are simply not important.*

In the light of Jesus Christ it should be possible *to adopt a different basic attitude,* to reach a different awareness, to gain another approach to life, in order to perceive the limitations of thinking in terms of achievement, in order to avoid the mania for efficiency and to break through the pressure of achievement, to become really free.

c. **What is important:** Not only are man's positive, fine, and good achievements unimportant in the last resort. The consoling aspect of the same message is that there are also negative, evil, and ugly "achievements" of man—and how much does everyone "achieve" in this respect, even if he is not precisely a sinful tax-collector. And these negative achievements, fortunately, are equally irrelevant in the last resort. Ultimately, with all man's unavoidable deeds and omissions, what counts is something different: *that, in both good and evil, man never under any circumstances gives up his absolute trust in God.*

What is the source of this certainty? The Crucified, absolutely passive, no longer capable of any achievement, and yet in the end justified by God in face of the defenders of pious works, is and remains God's living sign that the decision depends not on man and his deeds but—for man's welfare in both good and evil—on the merciful God who expects an unshakable trust from man in his own passion. It is then in the light of Jesus as the Crucified that man gains his certainty.

d. **Justification by faith:** In this way man is justified not only in his achievements and roles but in his whole existence, in his being human, quite independently of his achievements. He knows *that his life has a meaning:* not only in successes but also in failures, not only with brilliant achievements but with lapses, not only with increasing but also with declining efficiency. His life then makes sense even if, for any reason, he should not be accepted by his milieu or by society. That is what faith means: that, healthy or sick, able to work or unable to work, strong in achievement or weak in achievement, accustomed to success or passed over by success, guilty or innocent, not only at the end but throughout his whole life, a person clings absolutely and unshakably to that trust. If then, in all his human weakness, his hymn of praise, his "Te Deum" is addressed to the one true God and not to the false gods—money, pleasure, power, success—he can make bold also to refer the end of this hymn in any situation of himself: "In you, Lord, I have hoped; I shall never be brought to shame."

Instead of a Postscript[1]

Can a Catholic theologian with my views stay in the Catholic Church? This is a question that is continually being discussed on all sides. Will you permit me a personal observation on this occasion? Today, October 10, 1974, at this very moment, in the Roman church of St. Ignatius, Cardinal Döpfner is ordaining to the priesthood of the Catholic Church eleven students of the Pontifical German College. Call it chance if you will, since I did not myself choose the day and hour for this press conference, but it was exactly twenty years ago today, October 10, 1954, at this very hour, in the same Roman church of St. Ignatius of Loyola, as a student at the same pontifical college, that I myself was ordained priest of the Catholic Church. And, since I have maintained my loyalty and fidelity to this Church, working, studying, and fighting for it, although inevitably and constantly criticizing it, throughout these twenty years, you will perhaps understand now what I have to say. To put it very bluntly, I am utterly weary of continually protesting that I intend to stay in this Catholic Church and that my reasons for doing so are found in the gospel. In my new book I have explained all this once more. In any case, after twenty years, I feel no less Catholic than on the day of my ordination: a fact which does not exclude but indeed includes justified Protestant demands.

I must add this at once. The fact that today, after twenty years, I am not working in a parish, as I wanted to do at that time, but in an academic teaching post, for which I felt no strong urge, may likewise be regarded as accidental. My pastoral intentions, even now when I have had to work as a university teacher and scholar for fifteen years in Tübingen, have remained the same as they were when I was chaplain to the domestic staff at the German College in Rome, later curate in Lucerne, and priest-warden in Münster, Westphalia. My work, then, is that of a theologian whose prosaic and very arduous task is "theo-logy," "talk about God": how it is possible to speak of God in the world of today so that people do not simply repeat what has been said without understanding it but really do understand it.

And not any sort of theology, but a "Christian" theology: how it is possible to speak of this Jesus Christ so that people do not merely repeat traditional Christian formulas but are able to live and act convincingly in the light of the Christian message in society today. Theology, that is, understood as a "service" to men, who, as we are becoming more and more aware in modern material needs.

Twenty years of theology have gone into this book. Despite the first press reports, it is not a "Look Back in Anger" but a realistically sifting look forward. I am not taking stock of the twenty years: I have no theological past to master. The book is a processing of twenty years of work during which it slowly became clearer to me what being human and being Christian can mean, in the light of the gospel, for man at the present time. This book, undoubtedly critical in many respects, is not written against Rome: It is even written for Rome—and for the World Council of Churches. It is written to defend and justify, to clarify and stimulate Christian faith and life at a time when the churches have unfortunately lost rather than gained in credibility. It seeks to bring to light for this present time the original Christian message and particularly the figure of Jesus of Nazareth. It does not, of course, merely seek to proclaim, declaim, or declare in theological terms. It seeks to provide reasons: to show that even someone with a critical mind can justify, to his reason and to those around him, his being a Christian, and why he can do so. Perhaps this book will now finally discredit the cheap clichés about Küng as destructive critic of the Church, hostile to the pope, demolisher of dogmas. This book seeks to do no more and no less than to give people the courage to be Christians.

Certainly, critical in spirit, this book leaves nothing unquestioned, but it presses forward through all the negative criticism to positive answers. And, since it aimed at scrutinizing as exhaustively as possible and—at decisive points—at distinguishing and interpreting as precisely as possible, it could not be short. It deals with material that is found elsewhere in several volumes.

Do not expect therefore any cheap sensations from this book. The real sensation is what this Jesus of Nazareth himself, in his words, deeds, and fate, has to say about God and man here and now for the individual and for society. Is it then simply another book about Jesus? Not at all. But where then does its originality lie? Certainly not in all that had to be said in it about miracles, authentic and unauthentic sayings of Jesus, virgin birth and empty tomb, ascension to heaven and descent into hell, the founding of the Church and the complexity of the constitution of the New Testament Church, and everything else that could have been gathered long ago from the works of leading Protestant and Catholic exegetes—if anyone wanted to do so.

The originality lies elsewhere. In this book an attempt is made:

• not only to tackle particular questions and particular fields of theology but to present the Christian message as a whole against the background of modern ideologies and religions, in a comprehensive, consistent synthesis worked out uniformly and systematically down to the last detail, as it must be attempted by an individual particularly in view of the specialization of theological studies;

• tell the truth fearlessly and impartially, regardless of ecclesiastical politics and undisturbed by theological confrontations and fashions; an uncurtailed theological criticism, based on up-to-date scholarship and intellectually honest arguments, linked with an unshakable confidence in the Christian cause;

• consequently to start out not from theological man's wide-ranging and complex questions, and in the light of these to press on with all the abundance of information in increasingly close concentration to the heart of the Christian faith, so that what is human, what is universally religious and outside the Church, is taken more seriously than otherwise and yet at the same time what is distinctively Christian is more clearly set out and the essential separated from the nonessential;

• to speak the language of modern man, without biblical archaisms or scholastic dogmatisms, but also without the jargon of trendy theologians; making the greatest possible effort to speak simply and to formulate our arguments intelligibly but also precisely, discriminatingly, and impressively for those of our contemporaries who have no previous theological training:

• on the basis of personal research ranging from the doctrine of justification to Christology and ecclesiology, to integrate also denominational differences and thus to set out what is common to the Christian denominations as a renewed appeal finally for practical organizational agreement; not a new theory alongside others but the basic consensus possible today, not only between the Christian churches but also between the more important theological trends;

• on the basis of exegetical and historical studies, in fundamental theology, in dogmatics and ethics, and finally in practical theology, to give expression to the other scarcely perceptible unity of theology from the question of God to the question of the Church, in such a way that it is impossible to overlook the inviolable connection between credible theory and livable practice, between individual and society, criticism of the age and criticism of the Church, personal devotion and institutional reform.

In order to avoid any possible misunderstanding, I would like to say in conclusion: As author of this aid to being a Christian for modern man, I do not by any means consider myself a model Christian. I shall therefore be content to quote a single sentence from the book: "This book was written, not because the author thinks he is a good Christian, but because he thinks that being a Christian is a particularly good thing."

Translated by EDWARD QUINN

NOTE

1. Press conference at the Frankfurt Book Fair, October 10, 1974, on the occasion of the publication of *Christ sein*. This press conference was originally translated for *The Tablet,* London, October 19, 1974, and appears now, slightly revised, by permission of the editor.

PART TWO

I. The Christian in Society

A Conversation

Blessed are you who are poor, for yours is the kingdom of God. Blessed are you who are now hungry, for you will be satisfied. Blessed are you who are now weeping, for you will laugh. Blessed are you when people hate you, reject you, insult you, denounce your name as evil, on account of the Son of Man. Rejoice on that day and exult for joy, for see how great will be your reward in heaven. For their ancestors did the same to the prophets.

But woe to you who are rich, for you have had your consolation. Woe to you who are now satisfied, for you will be hungry. Woe to you who are now laughing, for you will mourn and weep. Woe to you when all speak well of you, for their ancestors did the same to the false prophets.

But to you who are listening I say: Love your enemies, do good to those who hate you, bless those who curse you, pray for those who calumniate you. To the man who strikes you on one cheek, present the other cheek too; to the man who takes your cloak from you, do not refuse your tunic.

These words are found in Luke's Gospel, chapter 6, verses 20 to 29. They are spoken by Jesus in the Sermon on the Mount and are addressed to the people listening there. They are addressed to Christians of all times. Also to those living today. The present discussion centers on the resurrection and on this Sermon on the Mount.

Doubts about miracles

EX LIBRIS: In the twentieth chapter of John's Gospel we read how Thomas questions the story of Jesus' resurrection from the dead as related by the other disciples. It is only when Jesus himself appears and invites him to touch the wounds of the crucifixion that Thomas believes in the miracle of the resurrection. Jesus then says to him: "You believe because you can see me. Happy are those who have not seen and yet believe." From Thomas onwards doubts about Jesus' resurrection and the other miracles have never died down, even among theologians. Does faith without sight mean in the Bible knowledge of the indemonstrable? And is this faith the precondition of being a Christian in the world?

PROFESSOR KÜNG: First of all, what does "faith" not mean? Certainly faith is not demonstrable, any more than love. But neither is faith irrational, unreasonable, again any more than love. We should not regard faith a priori as purely an act of the intellect. It is not a question merely of theoretical knowledge: neither—as often among Protestants—of accepting as true (infallible) biblical texts nor—as with some Catholics—of accepting as true (infallible) statements of the Church. Still less does faith mean an assent to more or less improbable, unintelligible, or even absurd assertions.

If faith were understood in this way, in the last resort it would be an unreasonable, arbitrary act: a voluntary decision based on inadequate understanding, an unconsidered risk, an unjustifiable leap, perhaps no more than a simple duty of obedience. But this would be unworthy of man as a being endowed with reason—more than ever in modern times when we want to test everything critically and to understand it correctly.

Act of trust

EX LIBRIS: But that is just how faith has been understood and even today is still understood by many. How otherwise do you define faith?

KÜNG: To put it briefly, faith is an act of trust. And this is an entirely reasonable action: We understand what we believe. But at the same time it is more than a rational action. In faith—as again in love —we commit ourselves to something which is more than reason. Can I ever adopt any other attitude to that mysterious, ultimate reality which is also the primal reality and which we designate by the name "God"? We do not see God. He is not evident. He is not palpable. If he were, he would not be God. This ultimate reality can be accepted only on trust: by committing myself absolutely, as a whole human being with all the powers of my mind, to the fact that this utterly final and utterly primal reality—before even the first atoms of hydrogen—exists and means something decisive for my life and death. Hence faith is at one and the same time an act of knowing, willing, and feeling: a basic trust in regard to God himself, which certainly includes an acceptance of certain truths.

EX LIBRIS: It is true that Jesus said many things which provoke precisely this trust in God. But, with all that he said, demanded, and lived, would he have been less significant if he had not risen, if he had not healed the sick and raised the dead? Can we not believe in God without miracles?

KÜNG: Christian faith is not primarily faith in miracles. For faith in miracles can also mean a craving for miracles. The latter exists in all religions and—in all the varied forms of superstition—even among nonreligious people. "Miracles" in the true sense—that is, charismatic deeds in the form of signs—Jesus produced in two ways, as even the most critical historians admit. In the first place he cured the sick and also expelled demons: he healed the psychically ill, such as epileptics, illnesses at that time generally associated with demons. Other miracles, in particular nature miracles like walking on the lake, in the light of the present state of research cannot without more ado be regarded as historical facts. But even Jesus' genuine charismatic deeds are not unequivocal arguments of credibility which could be used as proofs of faith. In themselves such deeds are ambiguous: Even Jesus' contemporaries attributed them not to God but to the devil. They are not proofs but pointers. It is only in the light of Jesus' words that his significant deeds acquire an unequivocal meaning and are seen to be rightly interpreted as salvation-deeds. There is a long chapter also on this difficult question in my book *On Being a Christian*.

Dying into the ultimate reality

EX LIBRIS: What then is the point of Jesus' resurrection from the dead? Was it meant to convince the Pharisees that Jesus was in fact the Messiah?

KÜNG: Jesus' resurrection is not just one sort of miracle among others. This it cannot be if only because we are not concerned here with an event in the life of Jesus. What is really involved is that which constitutes the end of human life—that is, death—which in every case raises the question of what it is into which man dies. Does he simply die into nothingness? Or is there a reality other than the reality of this life? Does he then die into another, an ultimate reality?

The answer of Christian faith runs: Jesus and—looking to him— we too die not into nothingness but into an absolutely final, most real reality, which we call "God." Hence it is not a matter of indifference whether we accept Jesus as taken up to God and into his life ("resurrection," "ascension") or see the work of Jesus as a fiasco ending in nothing. Only in the light of Jesus' new life with God was his message and work seen to be authenticated and confirmed by God; only in this light can that message demand an ultimate commitment which the word of man alone cannot demand. Only when the requirements of this Jesus of Nazareth are seen as the requirements of God himself do they become an absolute obligation for the believer. In my book I deal at some length with the fact that we may not of course confuse the Easter message of the new life with God with the frequently inconsistent Easter stories, which were developed in a legendary style even in New Testament times. Basically the Easter message means only the one thing that all the New Testament documents unanimously attest: This crucified Jesus of Nazareth lives through and with God, as a hope for all men.

Blessed are the poor

EX LIBRIS: We can certainly describe the Sermon on the Mount as the heart of the gospel message. It contains at the beginning the declaration of the happiness of the poor, of those who are hated and rejected by men. Are these the conditions required for sharing in the kingdom of God?

KÜNG: They are certainly not preconditions in the juridical sense. This is just what is notable about the Sermon on the Mount: that it does not begin like so many sermons with legal requirements—"You must now," "You shall now"—but with promises—"blessed are you who . . ." It is in fact evident that the promises we human beings make—for instance, "Happy the man who gets to the top," "who has a lot of money," "who is healthy"—do not in themselves create happiness. On the other hand, we see that with Jesus there is a promise of happiness even for the poor, the unhappy, the sick, the unsuccessful. This is the surprising thing: that there is a promise also and particularly for the unhappy, those who weep, who are hungry and without hope; that these are the very ones primarily addressed and given hope by Jesus. And who is there who is not jointly addressed here?

EX LIBRIS: But this too can be abused, as when the Church or some other authority puts off the poor in this world by promises of what is to come, of the hereafter.

KÜNG: True. But the promises in the gospel should not be so distorted. The Beatitudes are not meant to rouse enthusiasm as a way of escape from the difficulties of the present life and of society today. But they are meant to show that unhappiness, poverty, failure, tears, and death are not final, that all men even now are promised happiness, and that the better end makes it possible already to see the sad present in a different way and to master it. For the person who knows all this—and Jesus himself said a great deal on the subject—can also even in the present life master poverty, sickness, and failure; in another sense and by this very fact become truly man. This is not guaranteed if he worships only success, money, and health as the highest values.

Woe to you rich . . .

EX LIBRIS: How are we to understand the "Woes" in the Sermon on the Mount, addressed to the rich, to those who are satisfied, laughing, and respected. In the story of the rich young man Jesus says that the kingdom of God presents difficulties to the rich, that it is easier for a camel to get through the eye of a needle than for a rich man to enter the kingdom of God. What does this mean in the year 1975?

KÜNG: Whether people in 1975 like it or not, there is no doubt that Jesus himself was poor and a partisan of the poor. "Poor" at any rate in the very widest sense of the term, as it is also said in the Sermon on the Mount: the mourners, the hungry, the failures, the powerless and insignificant. He sets up as shocking examples the rich who want to serve two masters, God and mammon: all those people who give their hearts not to God but to things which rust and moth can consume and thieves steal. Money cannot be a god alongside the true God. Jesus clearly brings out the fact that wealth in this sense is extremely dangerous for man's salvation. Poverty on the other hand in itself is not evil or shameful.

Jesus' partisanship of the poor however is not romantic enthusiasm. He does not propagate dispossession of the rich, any kind of dictatorship of the proletariat, any revenge on the exploiters, any expropriation of the expropriators, the oppression of the oppressors. On the contrary he demands peace and renunciation of power. Nor did he demand—like the Jewish sect of the Essenes in the monastery at Qumran in his time—the surrender of one's possessions to a community. Anyone who renounces his property is not to transfer it to common ownership but must give it to those who have less than he has.

EX LIBRIS: But the first Christians sold their possessions and gave the proceeds to the community. Each received according to his needs and everyone was happy. Ananias and Sapphira had to die because they had deceived the community about the price received from the sale of their possessions and wanted to keep a part of it for themselves. There was also a kind of Christian communism, which must mean at least that this is not to be excluded as a possibility for the Christian life.

KÜNG: A possibility, but not a necessity. The history of the primitive Church was idealized at an early date. Certainly Jesus himself never required his supporters simply to renounce ownership. Individual sayings—and indeed the whole Sermon on the Mount—are not to be understood as law. What Jesus demanded of the rich young man—to set out with him—he never demanded in a general way and rigidly in every situation. Hence it would be wrong to construct an economically naive Christianity from these premises, even perhaps making a virtue of necessity and giving to poverty a religious trimming. For need teaches people not only to pray but also to curse.

Jesus does not glorify poverty, does not offer any opium; nor can the modern Church and its preachers do so. Poverty, suffering, and hunger are misery and not present bliss. We may not therefore make a mental leap, remaining spiritually aloof in face of injustice, but we must fight it with all our human resources. The poor must not be put off with cheap promises of compensation hereafter. But, according to Jesus, neither is poverty to be abolished overnight by force in a fanatical revolutionary effort—mostly only creating more misery. Jesus does not preach any rancor against the rich; he has no wish to be one of those violent benefactors of the people who merely continue to twist the spiral of force and counterforce, instead of breaking through it.

EX LIBRIS: But by placing himself decisively on the side of the poor and accusing the rich, he brought down on himself the hatred of the powerful. . . .

KÜNG: Obviously Jesus did not agree with the existing social conditions nor with their defenders. But he does not see the final solution in the same way as those who want to change society by revolution. He shows a different way and calls to the poor in the midst of their misery at the present time: "Blessed, happy are you."

Do not be anxious

EX LIBRIS: And for us who are alive today what does this mean: no glorifying of poverty?

KÜNG: For us Christians today this means the strict requirement of inner freedom from possessions: a "poverty in spirit" which must be realized differently in different situations. It is clear too from the Gospels that different people in Jesus' circle dealt with their possessions in different ways. One has everything, another has given half his property away, a third has kept his possessions and is thus able to help—and Jesus recognized the different forms of internal freedom from possessions.

EX LIBRIS: How can inner freedom from possessions become effective and visible today?

KÜNG: According to Jesus this inner freedom from possessions has to make itself felt especially in two respects—and this is of the greatest importance in particular for people in the efficiency-oriented, consumer society of today. First the basic attitude of frugal simplicity which makes it possible not to be demanding, presumptuous, or arrogant—and this is possible for the economically rich and the economically poor. Secondly, the basic attitude of confident unconcern: In the midst of all our inescapable cares, we are not anxiously concerned about the morrow. Today it is more urgent than ever not to be constantly tormenting ourselves and continually asking, "What shall we eat, what shall we drink, with what shall we be clothed?"

EX LIBRIS: Then we are hardly exemplary Christians if we read the newspapers and listen to the politicians. As soon as the economy begins to slow down, we become very anxious about the morrow.

KÜNG: But it is just in both the world economic difficulties and the smaller difficulties of individual families and firms that this deeper confidence should not be given up. It is especially important to be able to rise above these difficulties at times of economic strain. People who base their life and work on faith and trust in something other than merely material reality and the values of this world are also differently equipped to master constructively the difficulties of this real world in which we live.

EX LIBRIS: Do not be anxious. Are not the birds in the air and the lilies in the field supposed to be our examples?

KÜNG: True. But this must not be understood naively. These images require us to dissociate ourselves from our own possessions, to take care that possessions do not come between God and men, nor between man and his fellow men; they require us to become and remain capable, without envy or ambition, with all that we have, of existing for others, of renouncing something for the other person, so that we do not prove to be slaves of our possessions but try to use them to serve others.

The happiness of serving

EX LIBRIS: Francis of Assisi set up a sign. Certain monastic orders too—the Carthusians, for example—once set up signs of the possibility of renunciation. Are these signs still effective today?

KÜNG: That depends. Religious orders can certainly be signs in this sense, if they do not pile up goods and thus practice a kind of collective capitalism. I have known communities and members of religious orders in all parts of the world living in the utmost simplicity and thus performing a service to men: in the Church's proclamation and theology, in practical works of charity, in nursing the sick and in pastoral care, in every possible type of social work. In this connection nuns especially deserve to be mentioned for the splendid example of selfless service and renunciation which they give in countless hospitals in our own country and in the world at large. In all this people can often be seen to be experiencing something of the happiness promised in the Beatitudes, as a result of committing themselves for their fellow men in the light of Jesus' message.

On the other hand, it must be observed that Jesus was not an ascetic like John the Baptist. His message does not aim at monastic asceticism expressed in as many special achievements as possible. We must not preach the Christian gospel in such a way as to suggest that someone is less of a Christian if he tries to serve God and men quite normally in a secular calling while living with his family. A vocation to the religious life, to a specific commitment, is a special grace. But every father, every mother, devoting themselves to their children and their fellow men, are equally fulfilling in their own way the message of Christ.

In the last resort the important thing is whether we live for ourselves in a selfish way or for our fellow men who are living with us. Love of neighbor becomes the criterion for love of God. Not only for religious, but for anyone in any situation, it is possible to maintain an attitude of unconcern and unpretentiousness, of inner freedom from possessions.

Love your enemies

EX LIBRIS: In the Sermon on the Mount Jesus postulates love of enemies. We are to do good to those who hate us. If someone strikes us on the right cheek we should offer him the left also. We should not judge and condemn, but forgive. Jesus thinks these requirements can be fulfilled: If anyone hears them and acts accordingly, he is building his house on a rock; if anyone does not act in this way, he is building on sand. But is it really possible to fulfill them? Is it not asking too much of people? Is not love of enemies contrary to man's nature?

KÜNG: Certainly it is not so obviously, so specifically human as some non-Christian humanists think. Jesus' demands are undoubtedly uncompromising and radical. He does not give merely casuistic advice on how to get through in the particular case. He makes absolute demands because to him God's will itself seems absolute and for him it is quite clear that God's will means man's well-being. He draws his conclusions in the light of this. But again these requirements may not be understood as universal, comprehensive moral principles and directives for all questions of life. Jesus has no wish to be a legislator. He does not bind people to the old legal system, nor does he set up a new law for all spheres of life. He did not compose either a moral theology or a code of conduct. What he wants is to make people aware of what is decisive for human life by simple examples, appeals, and directives, expressed often in an exaggerated Eastern style, regardless of ifs and buts.

EX LIBRIS: What is this decisive element?

KÜNG: It is obedience to God's will in every situation, always aiming at the comprehensive well-being of our fellow man, the one who needs me at this very moment, our "neighbor." It is love of God and neighbor. For Jesus—and this is typical of him—this love of neighbor would not be radical if it were not kept up consistently to the very end, even to include people who are opposed to ourselves: our opponents, our enemies.

For our time

EX LIBRIS: It is just here that Jesus formulates very clearly, vividly, and concretely, what must be done: If someone strikes us, we are not to resist. Can we simply say that this is not to be taken literally?

KÜNG: These requirements too must constantly be transposed into our modern world. Even in Jesus' time they did not mean an effusive love. They have nothing to do with feelings or a euphoric "embrace for the millions" as in Schiller's *Ode to Joy*. Love means benevolence. Despite all objective antagonisms, I do not hate the man who is my opponent, perhaps even truly my enemy; I do not want to liquidate him, even if I were able to do so. It means that I try to approach him with a sincere, active benevolence in order to win him over instead of repelling him.

In the individal case this is often difficult. And yet it is quite possible for anyone to learn from experience that he can live in accordance with these requirements even today. In a political, professional, or family conflict I can say, "I'll get rid of that fellow if I can manage it." But, despite all objective severity—which, of course, Jesus also displayed—I can carry on the conflict, often unavoidable, in a spirit of real benevolence so that the other person can say to himself, "For all his commitment to his cause, in the last resort, he does not wish evil to me but good." This is something very great. Many a conflict has been settled in this way and many another even prevented. And that is why one of the Beatitudes also runs: "Blessed are the peacemakers."

EX LIBRIS: This again is an issue which is very real, important also for the world.

KÜNG: This requirement is not directed only at individuals. As far as Christians are involved, it ought increasingly to determine also social life and politics on the grand scale.

EX LIBRIS: It seems that not many Christians are involved.

KÜNG: Perhaps more than we think, whether known or unknown. Men like Dag Hammarskjöld and Martin Luther King—even Gandhi —have been active in politics in the spirit of the Sermon on the Mount. Helder Camara is another. But there are also countless other men and women in public life, giving expression unobtrusively to these Christian convictions. And they do more for their group, their country, and humanity as a whole than those who seek popularity by running down and disparaging their political opponents, the other party, the other economic group, the other country, and thus lead to disastrous polarizations and hate-filled antagonisms. Sooner or later it all ends in wars, great or small, hot or cold, at the expense of human beings.

EX LIBRIS: It is just at this point that the question arises whether politicians calling themselves Christians and perhaps even members of a party calling itself Christian do not make it too easy for themselves by declaring so definitely that the Sermon on the Mount cannot be applied to politics, that it is concerned only with the private life of the individual. Can we make such a neat distinction between the Christian and the politician? Can we listen to what is said about love of enemies in the church on Sunday and start lashing into our political opponents again first thing on Monday morning?

KÜNG: It is not the Christian label but the Christian deed which is decisive for being a Christian. We read in Scripture, "If someone *does* my words, he will know that they are the truth." This is not a truth we can appropriate purely theoretically and then give it expression in an organized way, like a system of political economy or sociology. It is a message which challenges the individual in his freedom, no matter what his party or group, which invites him: "Have a try." And if he makes the attempt for himself, he can learn that this message is true, since it proves to be true in his concrete case: It has stood the test of practice.

Neopaganism

EX LIBRIS: It was just because Jesus demanded love of enemies that Friedrich Nietzsche described him as a manifestation of decadence. One has the impression that many politicians and in particular many industrialists agree with Nietzsche, even if they do not admit it.

KÜNG: It would be possible to say a great deal both for and against Nietzsche. In fact, he spoke with great respect about Jesus himself and concentrated his attack properly speaking and mainly on Christianity, the Church and the priests. But, particularly by his glorification of the strong, the hard, and pitiless, he did a great deal to supply the National Socialists with the ideology which demonstrated the "greatness of man" by reference to a "leader" and to "master-men" who were anything but Christians; but they were also anything but truly great men, still less supermen. Politicians, employers, and trade unionists who defend indiscriminately hardness, individual or collective selfishness, and strong personalities in the political and economic struggle today are putting into practice what is essentially a neopagan view. They should recall what a mess this sort of neopaganism has already gotten us into in this century. But do we not find today some genuine realists in particular who demand a different approach to life, a different basic attitude, a different scale of values, different priorities, for the sake of man's true well-being? I have said more about all this in *On Being a Christian*.

Misunderstandings about the Sermon on the Mount

EX LIBRIS: Even in politics it is often only individuals, even isolated individuals, who attempt to realize the spirit of the Sermon on the Mount. I would add to those mentioned by you the name of Kurt Scharf, Bishop of Berlin, who visited Ulrike Meinhof in prison and on that account had to put up with some very harsh criticism—again from Christian politicians—just as Jesus faced criticism from the Pharisees when he did not turn away the woman known as a sinner in the city but allowed her to anoint his feet. Thus the Sermon on the Mount is really an invitation to the individual in his practical life and not primarily a directive and criterion for society, since society can be bound perhaps to a minimum of legal requirements but not to a maximum of moral requirements.

KÜNG: The Sermon on the Mount can be misunderstood in two respects. The first misunderstanding consists in regarding it as a concrete outline of a new social order of love and peace to be observed literally: that is, as a kingdom of Christ which can be realized here and now on earth, which does not need any political power or legal system, police or army, as—for example—Leo Tolstoy and certain religious socialists have maintained.

The other, no less serious misunderstanding is to assume that the Sermon on the Mount concerns only the individual, that it is relevant only to personal and family interests.

On all this it must be said that, even though the Sermon on the Mount gives no directions as to what a modern political and economic system should look like—which it simply is not meant to do— its consequences for society cannot be overlooked. In this society there are in fact conditions of injustice, oppression, and dehumanization, which must be exposed and opposed. There are cases where we must commit ourselves and act out of a more demanding love even more than merely out of a sense of justice. That is, although the Sermon on the Mount cannot simply be expanded into a social program, neither can it be reduced merely to rules applicable to the situation of the individual or the family. Undoubtedly it is addressed primarily to the individual. But the individual should take his stand on the Sermon on the Mount also in industry and trade, in politics, in cultural affairs, wherever he is active. And this then has social consequences.

EX LIBRIS: Can you give examples?

KÜNG: To do that, we would have to write not only a history of the Church but a history of Christianity. I am thinking, for instance, of what has been realized in the field of nursing as a result of the systematic organization of care for the sick in hospitals and homes— which did not happen in any other religion. I recall the influence of the Sermon on the Mount on a new order of peace to replace the private wars of the Middle Ages. There are similar attempts today. We have "Pax Christi" and other movements for nonviolence, for racial equality, for social justice and the protection of minorities. All these are movements striving indirectly to realize the requirements of the Sermon on the Mount in society. They are important initiatives both on the small and on the grand scale. Even though they cannot be taken as substitutes for political and economic systems, it is from such movements, groups, and individuals that new stimuli constantly emerge with consequences that cannot yet be foreseen or measured.

New human beings

EX LIBRIS: These initiatives, then, are both more and less than programs of political and economic-social reform?

KÜNG: The Christian message begins at the point which no state constitution, no economic, social, or cultural system can really reach: the point at which man experiences a change of heart, at his personal center. This is what politicians, economists, and sociologists desire but do not achieve, what Karl Marx also demanded in vain: "a new human being." But the renewal of man can come only from his personal center. From that center he acquires a different basic attitude to life, a different life style; it is there that he sets up different priorities in his life, another measure of what is important, so that the very palpable economic values in particular are no longer regarded as supreme. This is what the Sermon on the Mount and indeed the Christian message as a whole demands, promises, offers, and makes possible: what then can have and in fact has had direct and very diverse effects even within the social field.

The Church and love of enemies

EX LIBRIS: Where does the Church stand in regard to the requirements of the Sermon on the Mount? The Church claims to be the community of believers, oriented to the kingdom of God. But its powerful machinery makes it an influential secular power. It carries on politics, as states carry on politics. It has amassed great wealth; it owns banks: hence it does not despise economic values. It has often judged and condemned. When struck, it has not always offered the other cheek; it has even occasionally destroyed its enemies—and, indeed, with fire and sword. It has not always taken the side of the poor and outcasts as unequivocally as Jesus did, but it has certainly often been on the side of the rich and powerful against the oppressed. And I am not thinking here only of the Catholic Church but also of the Protestant ecclesial communities. There were times when the Reformed churches were perhaps more decidedly than the Catholic Church on the side of the powerful.

But the question does inevitably arise here as to whether the Church is not almost inevitably bound to become a secular power and act according to secular standards if it gives itself secular structures, if it amasses wealth, if it builds up hierarchies tied in fact to the use of power. Is it not—so to speak—automatically placed in the position of the rich young man who could not bring himself to abandon his possessions?

KÜNG: This is unfortunately one aspect of the churches, for they are composed of human beings and not of angels. It is unfortunate that the churches and their representatives for a long time have not always been credible heralds of the kingdom of God, credible witnesses for the cause of Jesus Christ, for which they were supposed to stand. Nor, of course, can any member of the Church assume that this observation does not apply to him. . . .

EX LIBRIS: On the contrary. If the members of the churches try to further the cause of Jesus Christ with the aid of party-political methods, then the spirit of love of neighbor or love of enemies will not always be realized.

KÜNG: In any case it is quite certainly not the Church's task to strive for a religio-political theocracy or any kind of seizure of power in society. Instead of setting up an empire of unspiritual power, it has the opportunity in the light of the message of Christ of exercising a ministry without compulsion or force—in other words, a service—by constantly standing up especially for socially neglected or despised groups for whom no one cares, by defending all who are despised or downtrodden, and yet at the same time considering impartially the cares of those who are known as "the ruling class."

Instead of setting up confrontation barricades, denominational, ideological, intellectual barriers, the Church ought to stand in all areas for peace and justice, against discord and all thinking in terms of friend against foe. Its message should assist people to control their defense mechanisms, to get away from their fixed roles, to approach each other and learn to understand each other. The Church therefore should not ally itself with one power or another against other people. It should never identify itself from the outset with any kind of secular grouping, a political party, a cultural association, an economic or social power group. It should never commit itself uncritically and unconditionally to a particular economic, social, cultural, political, philosophical, or ideological system. On the contrary, since its message is "radical" in the strict sense of the term, reaching to the "roots," it should be continually also disturbing, alienating, sometimes upsetting, and at any rate questioning with a liberating purpose all secular powers, parties, groupings, and systems. And on this account it will therefore be resisted and attacked. In this sense the Church cannot, any more than its Master, expect to gain an easy triumph. It should regard unco-operative outsiders in particular not as enemies to be hated, destroyed, harassed, but as its neighbors to be understood, borne with, indulged, and encouraged.

EX LIBRIS: The way which the Christian Church must follow is marked out in advance. But can it really follow that path as an institution, as an organization? Is it not obstructed by people who are Christians by baptism without being such at heart?

KÜNG: I am sure that, if a Church forgets that it exists for selfless, active service to society, to people and groups, and even to its opponents, it will lose its true dignity, its claim, and even the justification of its existence. For then it abandons its discipleship of him whom it seeks to serve. On the other hand, if a Church remains aware of the fact that what is to come is not itself but God's kingdom in "power and glory," it knows also that it is great without any display of power or use of force. Even if it is constantly ignored, neglected, or merely tolerated by society, in this position particularly it can render a service to mankind which no other institution, no political party, no trade union, and not even the state can undertake. Fortunately, it does this also in a way that is scarcely noticed, more in small things than in great, more at the "base" than at the hierarchical tip.

EX LIBRIS: And its aim is in fact to change man at his personal center and lead him to those values which are more than the ephemeral values of the world. . . .

KÜNG: It all amounts really to one thing. The churches should so present the Christian message as to show people increasingly how to live and act according to the standard of Christ in a truly human way, to suffer in a truly human way, and finally also to die in a truly human way. For man as an individual and in society is constantly sustained by God even in misery, suffering, and all that is negative, and throughout all that is negative he can be helpful to his fellow man.

Is the Christian a dissident or heretic?

EX LIBRIS: Since the Church in its history hitherto has constantly dissociated itself from Jesus' message in one point or another and will certainly continue to depart from it, does not being a Christian then often mean being a dissident, a heretic, not only in face of the world but also in face of an acclimatized Church?

KÜNG: Jusus did not require people to make martyrs of themselves. He did not expect us to seek conflict from the outset. But the fact cannot be overlooked that the Christian message is extraordinarily challenging and brings one continually into conflict with what is regarded as human and with those who do not want to act in a Christian way. When, for example, a Christian is prepared to follow the message of Jesus, to renounce the exercise of power or a sum of money without expecting compensation, there will always be those who regard all this as rather absurd. His action is ridiculed, his motives perhaps suspected, and occasionally there may be a hostile reaction. In this sense then such a Christian can in fact seem different from others who believe in the use of power. He may seem to have a different belief, to be in a sense a "heretic" within society and often even within his all-too-acclimatized Church.

On the meaning of life

EX LIBRIS: The relatives and family of a man like that will possibly get a psychiatric report drawn up on him. For what is contrary to the norm must in fact be abnormal.

KÜNG: We should not, however, deliberately try to be different. For this too can be a form of vanity. It is a question of trying simply, objectively, and straightforwardly, to live this Christian life as far as this is humanly possible and at the same time to make allowances from the outset for reactions of various kinds. For it must also be clear and clearly stated that acting in accordance with the message of Jesus produces also many friends, creates joy and agreement at the very point where they were not expected. In this sense trying to live the message of Jesus is by no means a grim duty but something wholly enjoyable. His message does not consist of threats but of good news. For it is only in this way that a genuine meaning enters at all into human life. If today young people in particular no longer find any meaning in life, this is mainly because society and parents— perhaps with the best intentions—have shown them the example only of taking up a calling with the greatest possible prospects, of getting to the top, of becoming rich. If no deeper meaning becomes apparent here, the overindulged younger generation rightly asks, "What is the point of all this?"

It should therefore be one of the main tasks of education to help young people learn from the very beginning that human life acquires a meaning only when we do not live for ourselves but get involved for others. They must learn that this can be done with good reason only if they are aware that they and the others are embraced and en- compassed by an invisible reality which is greater than themselves and greater than the others. This archetypal first and last, most real of all realities, which Jesus reveals, constitutes the primal meaning and final meaning of human living and dying, comprehending all provisional meanings: the goal of all goals.

May I myself end with a question?

In the present critical situation of the world and the churches are there not signs on all sides of a new approach? After many disap- pointments from ideologies on the right and on the left, can we not perceive a return to a truly Christian attitude to life, oriented to the new and better future? And this holds not only for the Soviet Union and the East, as Alexander Solzhenitsyn has urged, but also for the West, ruled as it is now by egoism, materialism, and nationalism.

It seems that there are some people from the most diverse camps and from different generations who are gaining a new understanding of all this. . . .

Interviewer: ALFRED A. HÄSLER
Translated by EDWARD QUINN

II. Jesus in Conflict: A Jewish-Christian Dialogue

Introduction

There have been many Jewish-Christian dialogues recently. For the most part however the decisive point has been left out, since there seemed to be no possibility of agreement on this. Here we have ventured to concentrate the dialogue directly on this decisive point: the Jew Jesus of Nazareth, who stands between Jews and Christians. We shall see how far we can get in this dialogue today if we carry it on in the light of the correct assumptions.

In the present dialogue, where both sides were wholly committed and which was heard by large numbers of radio listeners, there was neither victor nor vanquished. But neither did we come to the unsatisfactory "open end" which is the conclusion of so many similar discussions. Instead, a way was opened on which it will be worthwhile for both sides to continue, especially when there is more than an hour to spare for it. It resulted in real hope.

The dialogue was broadcast August 25, 1975, by Südwestfunk. We are grateful to Dr. Ludwig Klein, of Baden-Baden, for suggesting and arranging this broadcast. We are also grateful to Dr. Walter Strolz, of Freiburg im Breisgau, for leading the discussion. The printed version has been revised for grammar and style, but the content and character of the conversation remain unchanged.

Hans Küng / Pinchas Lapide
Tübingen–Jerusalem, October 1975

WALTER STROLZ: Dialogue is one of the typical features of the present intellectual and religious situation. It is carried on not only between different ideological camps but more especially between the different religions. A discussion between representatives of Judaism and of Christianity is not to be compared with dialogues carried on between the non-Christian world religions. The present dialogue has a *unique* significance. For Christianity, questioned about its origins, points back to Judaism in accordance with Romans 11:18: "You do not sustain the root, the root sustains you." A discussion on the question "Who is Jesus of Nazareth?" touches a living root of Christianity itself, reaching back to the history of Israel. It is natural then to ask, Dr. Lapide, what is your position in regard to the question "Who is Jesus of Nazareth?"

PINCHAS LAPIDE: My Judaism is "catholic" enough, in the original sense of the word, to find a place for both Spinoza and Jesus, for Philo and Flavius Josephus. I do not see why I should renounce a luminary of Judaism like the Rabbi of Nazareth, merely because some of the Christian images of Christ mean nothing to me. So much the more since I am aware of five bonds with Jesus which—if I may say so—perhaps bring him closer to me than to many a Christian theologian in Europe today.

Firstly, there is the setting in life. This includes both the geography and the topography, indeed the whole environment of the land of Israel, with its fauna and flora, its atmosphere and agriculture, the whole physical background of the Nazarene: This I know and this I share with him.

Secondly, the language. I speak Hebrew and think in this language, with Aramaic as a twin idiom. For me it is both the language of the country and also a sacred language of prayer and worship, just as it was for Jesus.

Thirdly, the understanding of the Bible. For him and for me the Hebrew Bible alone is sacred Scripture, which I acknowledge as such and which we both interpret according to rabbinical rules, which make it clear to us that every sentence in the Bible—as our Talmud so finely puts it—has seventy possible interpretations, and there is no Jewish pope to make a single exegesis into a dogma and declare the other sixty-nine heretical.

Fourthly, oriental imagination. This way of thinking finds expression in metaphors and parables and is averse to Western literalness, which places every word of Jesus under the microscope. The vine and the vineyard, the fig tree, the children of the kingdom, the wicked husbandmen, the prodigal son and—if you want—a hundred other metaphors of Jesus are straightforward allusions meant only for the Jew familiar with the Bible and for his ears. As soon as they are translated into Greek or—still more—into a modern European language, they sound not only strange but distorted and unnatural.

And *finally,* there is our concern for Israel. Just as formerly he had to fear for his people Israel, both because of the pagan powers externally and because of unbelief internally, so we—the faithful of Israel —fear today. Externally the danger is just as great as in the years A.D. 20 and 30 and internally unbelief threatens to de-Judaize many Jews. This anxious love for Israel with its thirst for redemption—I hope and believe—gives Jesus and myself a certain psychological solidarity.

WALTER STROLZ: We might then ask about this characterization of Jesus the Jew in his country and in its history: How was it possible for this *Jesus as Jew* to fade so much into the background for centuries in Christianity, in Christian theology and proclamation, so much so that we might say that he is regarded as an alien figure? Dr. Küng, what would you say to this?

HANS KÜNG: Obviously there is always a tendency to adapt such an exemplary figure, this Christ, whom we call the archetype, to our own standards. This is quite natural, for, seen as a whole, he is still very uncongenial. And he becomes more congenial for us if we fit him into our personal and social requirements, if we adapt him to our habits, our wishful thinking, our favorite notions. It is convenient for the ecclesiastical authorities to take Jesus—so to speak—as a man who even then wanted only to work with the religious establishment, to set up a higher morality. It is of course convenient also for the theologians simply to incorporate him into a theological system. And here I must say, Dr. Lapide, that I am deeply impressed by your brief recapitulation of what you as a Jew have in common with Jesus. Up to a point this is also what makes this Jesus alien to us Christians. His language itself is foreign to us. For us it always presents a linguistic and theological problem: The often double and triple translation and retranslation from a modern language into Greek and from Greek back into Hebrew or Aramaic. We have the same problem with the metaphors which he used. What you enumerated as common between you makes him alien to us Christians, but contemporary to you Jews. I am quite pleased that he cannot be appropriated by us in this way. And I think that you as Jews can help us to see him constantly in his originality and to discover him as a challenge for today.

WALTER STROLZ: I think we have reached the point, Dr. Küng, at which we must ask why the Church in the course of the history of

Christianity so often came between Jesus and Israel, why it broke down this original biblical relationship.

HANS KÜNG: To answer this we would have to relate the whole long history from the very beginning, since this process of detachment from the Jewish national community was inwardly founded in the profession of faith in Jesus as early as the first and second centuries. We would have to speak about the formation of a Gentile Christianity, free from the law. Then, unfortunately, we would have to speak of the sinister history—depressing even today—of Christians and Jews throughout the centuries. But I do not think there is much point in reopening here and now the history of anti-Judaism (a more accurate term than anti-Semitism): a history of blood and tears. This would be a theme for its own sake. To me it seems more important to bring out the fact—and I presume that my Jewish partner can also say something about this—that today conditions for a discussion are more favorable. At any rate it can be said of us, on the Christian side, that for a long time there has been a greater open-mindedness toward the Old Testament: that we must not only interpret it in a Christian way but also understand it independently of Christianity. We recognize today the importance of the rabbis for the New Testament and can understand it better in the light of their work. As Christians, also, we have ourselves compared Greek-Hellenistic thinking with Jewish and we can better appreciate today the stronger aspects of Hebrew thought: the keener sense of the latter for the great dynamism of history, for total orientation, its friendly attitude to the world and to the body, its hunger and thirst for justice, its orientation to the coming kingdom of God. I think then that all this has helped to overcome the Neoplatonic-Neoaristotelian-Scholastic-Neoscholastic encrustation of Christianity in the past. In any case, from the Second Vatican Council in the Catholic Church and also from the discussions on Christianity and Judaism in the World Council of Churches onwards, we have discovered again for ourselves the importance of Judaism for Christianity.

WALTER STROLZ: I also think, Professor Küng, that you have given a very apt description of the new open-mindedness of Christianity toward Judaism. Dr. Lapide, it would now be highly interesting to hear from you how as a Jew you regard this Christian open-mindedness today.

PICHAS LAPIDE: For eighteen hundred years the Church has done three things to Jesus: it has de-Judaized him, it has Hellenized him, and it has very effectively put us off him. This it has done by compulsory sermons, compulsory baptisms, kidnaping children—you know the rest as well as I do. As I see it, Christianity owes its foundation to the sublime image of Jesus in the primitive Church, in that Jewish community which saw in him, besides the prophet, a just man and a luminary of Israel or the Messiah—all mortal sons of Israel. As soon, however, as the young Gentile Church came gradually to make a god of him, Jewry tried by way of reaction to turn him into a devil. For a Savior–God who dies on the cross must—as Paul rightly said—be a scandal to the Jews, but not folly to the Gentiles. Here I would contradict Paul. For the Gentiles this was not folly but a supremely welcome entry into the community of salvation. And thus the two Jesus images grew apart until with the Monophysites Jesus became God in Christianity and in Judaism his name became taboo; the very mention of it was forbidden. It was only after Auschwitz that what I might call a rehumanizing of Jesus took place among Christians; it occurred as a result of a shift of emphasis to the *vere homo,* to the truly man, at a time when so few bipeds were real men. Jesus thus becomes an ideal man. And with the Jews he now comes out of the polemical hell of the entire Middle Ages back to the Judaism of his homeland. Brother Jesus is finally restored to his own as fellow man, as fellow Jew, as Israeli—it is not difficult to read all these interpretations into the Gospels—and even as Zionist and comrade in arms. We might almost say with Faust, "The tears are shed [and how many tears have not been shed!], he is earth's child again."

WALTER STROLZ: In connection with this observation, Professor Küng, I think it would be enlightening if you would briefly explain what Christian, and especially Catholic, theology have made of this rediscovery of the humanity of Jesus.

HANS KÜNG: It has at any rate become clear what has been far too much neglected hitherto in the dialogue between Christians and Jews. I am glad—and this itself is quite unusual for such a dialogue—that Rabbi Lapide was also prepared to talk precisely on this theme. Up to now Christians and Jews have really always talked only about generalities. And in this respect we must simply state that, if we talk merely in a general way about Christians and Jews and not about

Jews of Nazareth, we are overlooking precisely the real point of the controversy. The conflict between Christians and Jews is so serious because the rift goes through the Bible itself: We do indeed accept the Old Testament together with the Jews, but nevertheless we understand it in the light of the New and from this standpoint in the last resort interpret everything in the light of this Jew, Jesus of Nazareth: In this sense it is in fact, as you say, a question of the image we form for ourselves of Jesus.

I think that Christians should face your question as to whether they have rightly understood throughout the centuries this Jesus of Nazareth as he is originally attested in the New Testament. Or whether they have not perhaps dropped the originally Jewish element, whether they did not Hellenize him even at a very early stage. Did they not even put you off him—as you rather sharply but perhaps not entirely inaccurately expressed it—by all the coercive measures with which Christians tried to press and impose on Jews the message of Jesus as Messiah? I think, therefore, it has now become clear that the discussion here must be carried on in a different way, that it must concentrate particularly on this main point.

I want to add only one thing which, it seems to me, must give Jews also on their part something to think about. I am thinking, for instance, of the great Jewish painter Marc Chagall, who constantly represented the sufferings of his people in the image of the Crucified, and I wonder whether the history of this people can be understood differently and more deeply precisely from this standpoint: in the light of the Crucified who might almost stand as a personal symbol of Jewish history, the history of this people, a people with its God, a people of tears and of life, of plaint and trust. Could not Jesus then appear in this sense as a sign of Israel, crucified and risen?

At any rate, this—I think—is the question which ought to bring us together here in the discussion: Who is this Jesus of Nazareth? And I expect the Jew particularly to help the Christian to discover afresh the original Jesus. I imagine that this approach might lead to very many new ideas.

WALTER STROLZ: Dr. Lapide, we would be very grateful if you could answer this question, for it is connected with the experience of the continuity of Scripture, of biblical faith as a whole. I think that we have now reached a decisive point. We ought to ask what is the position of this Jesus in the total tradition of Scripture, of biblical revelation, and how far the Jew in particular can help us to reach a more

authentic understanding of Jesus: an understanding which brings
home to us afresh the continuity of salvation history.

PINCHAS LAPIDE: Here I would say that, for the Jews of my generation, ours is fundamentally a paschal self-understanding. It belongs
to Easter, because, for all Jews of our time, even for those who were
never in Europe, Auschwitz really means what Good Friday must be
for devout Christians: a Golgotha on a national scale. The foundation of the state of Israel, on the other hand, is Easter Sunday: the
resurrection from the ruins of the whole people, which finds its way
out of this mass Golgotha back to its biblical homeland, exactly as
twenty-seven prophecies in the Old Testament predict. For Jews who
were always persecuted, who were always the first victims of men's
injustice and want of love whenever world history was in the making,
who all too often had to bear the cross in which Christians believe,
who—despite all power and all violence—were able to endure as a
holy remnant: For this Jewish people what better embodiment could
you find than this poor rabbi of Nazareth? *Eli, Eli, lama sabachthani*
is not merely a psalm of David and a word of Jesus from the cross
but—I would almost say—the leitmotif of those who had to go to
Auschwitz and Majdanek. I received recently from New York photo-
copies of wills of Hasidic rabbis, drawn up on the eve of their de-
portation. *Eli, Eli, lama sabachthani* is the quintessence of these last
words of almost a whole generation of rabbis. Is not this rabbi,
bleeding on the cross, the authentic incarnation of his suffering
people: all too often murdered on the cross of this hatred of Jews
which we had to feel ourselves when we were young?

HANS KÜNG: Of course I would not like to have the fate of Jesus and
the fate of the Jewish people identified in an overly simple way. But I
think there is in fact a connection here. And I think it would be a
great help to Jewish-Christian dialogue—to put it very clearly—if on
your side, within Judaism, in the state of Israel and in world Jewry,
the rancor (undoubtedly understandable) or possibly mere skepticism in regard to this figure were broken down. What you have said
all points in this direction. I can certainly understand Jewish inhibi-
tions. I know an American rabbi who told me that his father always
spat out at the mention of this name, because it was the same name
which was invoked in all the Jewish pogroms they had had to endure
in Poland. A different attitude certainly involves an immense transformation. Dr. Lapide, do you yourself see in Israel and in Judaism,

in world Jewry as a whole, any signs that the former rejection, contempt, or even mere skepticism, are changing? And not only in the sense that people accept what I might call the "Jesus of culture," because he is—so to speak—a part of Western civilization, but also— if you want to express it in this way—the "Jesus of religion." Can you perhaps show me some kind of hopeful signs which make it clear that both sides are coming closer to each other here; that, if we Christians today understand the Old Testament better, you as Jews are also learning to understand the New Testament better?

PINCHAS LAPIDE: What I find particularly new in our time, in the last ten or fifteen years, is our mutual curiosity. Just as Christianity or—better—Christendom has never been so inquisitive, so anxious to learn something about its own Jewish roots, so too in the country of Israel there is emerging an almost equal curiosity to learn more about its Christian branches, for together we are really *one* tree of faith. And the twenty-nine Hebrew books on Jesus published in recent years which I analyzed in my book *Is This Not Joseph's Son?* have in common a sympathy and a love for the Nazarene which would have been impossible at any other time during the past eighteen hundred years—to be truthful, because of the Church.

We are very proud of our Einsteins, of our Heinrich Heines and Sigmund Freuds; we ought to be so much prouder of Jesus. But if Israel's most famous son has been passed over in silence for so long in Judaism, it is the fault of the Church—with its coercive measures, seeking to impose its faith by the sword, which simply will not work. Now, in the free mental climate of Israel, where there is neither Church coercion nor Christian pressure, we suddenly find a lively interest in the person of the Nazarene: an interest which is positive and without precedent in the whole of Jewish history. Speaking for our own generation, Dr. Küng, let us hope that this curiosity on your side and mine is a good omen for the future. If we in our generation can learn from one another, perhaps the next generation will do more.

WALTER STROLZ: The historico-concrete understanding of Jesus which Rabbi Lapide has just explained raises for you, Dr. Küng, the question as to how an understanding of Jesus from below might be strengthened within the Christian proclamation.

HANS KÜNG: Dr. Lapide has himself said that one of the three great difficulties in the way of discussion about Jesus is the Hellenization

or the very great transformation of the image of Jesus in the course
of centuries. I think that the difficulties of discussion on Jesus with
Jews—I would say the same of discussion with Muslims—are insur-
mountable if we simply begin with "You must make up your mind.
Is he God's Son or not?" Or even: "Is he God or not?" Yet this is
the way the question is mostly stated. Which means that the dialogue
is immediately at an end, before it has begun.

Of course, "from below" does not mean that we overlook or exclude God, for Jesus himself proclaims God's kingdom and God's
will. But "from below" means that we do not make ourselves equal
to God and consider everything, as it were, looking down from
heaven. It means considering Jesus and his history from an earthly
standpoint, from the standpoint of people of his own time, and asking, "What did people really see in him? How did Jesus' disciples understand him?" According to the Synoptic Gospels, he did not simply
come and say, "I am God's Son"; but he came and proclaimed God's
kingdom, God's will, proclaimed everything that we find attested particularly in these Gospels. These perspectives "from below," I think,
would make it possible to go together with the Jews for a good part
of the way, since they too can ask for their own part, "Who really
was he?"

PINCHAS LAPIDE: In other words, Dr. Küng, we can go on together
theologizing from below for thirty-three years—the whole span of
Jesus' earthly life—and that is no small thing. What really separate
us are forty-eight hours from the afternoon of the first Good Friday
onward. That means just two days, but they are, of course, the decisive days on which more or less the whole of Christology rests. But I
certainly would not underestimate thirty-three years, particularly as
there is still a great deal to be known which—in my opinion—has
not yet been investigated. Professor Küng, there are passages on
Jesus in the Talmud and in Midrash which, unfortunately, even up to
the present time have not been subjected to all the sciences of textual
criticism and from which some things might be gained in order to
construct a picture of Jesus which would bring home to us—to you
and me—the earthly Jesus as truly three-dimensional and credible.

HANS KÜNG: Certainly I would not have agreed with you so completely if you had concentrated exclusively on those two days. I do
agree with you if you say that in fact we know little about the thirty
years before his public activity, that even the infancy stories must not

simply be understood as historical records. It is only from the time of his appearance before John the Baptist that we know anything more definite. But I think it would be too simple if we were to maintain that a difference between Jesus and his contemporaries became evident only at the end. For the whole question is this: Why was there such a conflict at all? Why was Jesus not received differently by contemporary Jewry? Why in particular had he to be liquidated?

As Christians and Jews, however, we have so much in common. For Jews believe, as we do, in the coming of the kingdom of God. You too believe in all that has to be said in theological terms in the light of the Old Testament on what shapes history for good or bad. But it seems that at a very early stage—even at the very beginning, according to the oldest Gospel, that of Mark—a conflict arose between the Jew Jesus of Nazareth and certain—let us say, cautiously —Jewish circles. In this respect I have no desire simply to blame the Pharisees. I know that they appear in a very sinister light in the New Testament, not, however, entirely without reason. I am really interested in two points. Where do you see what is common, what Jesus evidently shared with the Jews of his own time, and where— secondly—do you see the difference?

PINCHAS LAPIDE: This is a very personal question. I have been considering it for thirty years. If you want it simplified, in a very brief form, I would say that Jesus presented to the Judaism of his time a harmony of contrasts, and both parts of this term make him for me primitively Jewish—I would almost say, only Jewish. You may ask why. It is certain that he was Jewish in spirit in at least six respects: in his hope, in his eschatology, in his Jewish ethos, in his blind trust in God, in his very Jewish messianic impatience, and—last but not least—in his Jewish suffering; this we can gather without difficulty from all four Gospels. The fact that he often presented a contrast with his milieu also makes him Jewish, for I know no luminary of Judaism from Moses onward who did not provoke lively opposition among the Jewish people.

We have no greater Jew than Moses. But read the book of Exodus and see how this Jewish people six times angered its leader and legislator, almost continually mutinied against him, and twice started rebellions in the desert which almost cost him his life. The same holds for a dozen other great Jews who much later—as with you in the Church—centuries after their death were canonized as "saints." The fact that Jesus set up a contrast, that he had enemies and opponents, this is one of the most striking proofs of his greatness—not of his non-Jewishness.

HANS KÜNG: Yes, but don't you see that this history becomes so dramatic, since it is precisely the figure of Moses who seems to stand between them: between Jesus, if you will, and his people. If only—like the prophets, invoking the authority of Moses—he had called people back to the true observance of the law; if only—like the rabbis, the legal experts, the theologians of his time—he had summoned people to a better observance of the law, then probably nothing would have happened. But the conflict between Jesus and, perhaps not necessarily his own people, but very definite and leading circles became so serious because they could not avoid the impression that he did not rely on that which hitherto had been the distinguishing mark of all Judaism, on that on which every Jew could rely, on what had united prophets, kings, and rabbinical scholars: that is, the unconditional acknowledgment of the law of God as God's holy will and in that sense therefore an obedience to the law which ought to be the aim also for the future.

For it was said at that time that, if on one day all these laws were fulfilled, in effect the fullness of time would have come, the kingdom of God could appear. And—to put it again in one sentence—I see the drama of this conflict precisely in the fact that in the last resort it was concerned with Moses, with the validity of the law, with that which really had to be the norm for man in everyday life.

PINCHAS LAPIDE: I'm terribly sorry to have to contradict you. But I want to make it crystal clear in one sentence. According to the three Gospels Matthew, Mark, and Luke, the Synoptic Jesus never and nowhere broke the law of Moses, the Torah of Moses, nor did he in any way provoke its infringement—it is entirely false to say that he did. With the Johannine Jesus there is only a single passage, and that is a borderline case: the healing on the Sabbath, where he says to the man who has been cured, "Take your bed and walk." Here there might be some discussion as to whether the law really was broken. But nowhere is there anything of the kind in Mark, Matthew, or Luke. And I must say that you Christians make it too easy for yourselves, because you take only the Pauline image of Jesus and assert that Jesus changed the law, rendered it invalid or even abolished it. This is not true. This is how Paul preached him to the Gentiles, but certainly not to the Jews, because he would otherwise have been thrown out of any synagogue at an early stage.

Neither Luke nor Mark nor Matthew, however, in their accounts of the action of Jesus assert that a single precept was ever infringed or still less broken. In this respect you must believe me, for I do know my Talmud more or less. What always surprises me is that at the end of the so-called "anti-Torah passages," at the end of the disputes, we read: "The people were amazed," or "The Pharisees were amazed." I am the person who is amazed, when I read this, for there is no cause for amazement here, although perhaps for admiration. This Jesus was as faithful to the law as I would hope to be. But I suspect that Jesus was more faithful to the law than I am—and I am an orthodox Jew.

HANS KÜNG: Well, I am glad that we have now taken a stand quite clearly on this decisive point. I would ask first of all whether there would have been any reason at all to liquidate him in this way if there had not already been a conflict on this point. And secondly, in the light not only of his condemnation but of the Gospels as a whole, can it be overlooked that Jesus' reaction to the law was in fact a wholly central and very problematic question? I would entirely agree with you—to avoid discussion of the wrong point—that he by no means wanted to abolish the law. Nor did he launch a frontal attack on the law by simply saying, "You don't need to observe it." It would certainly be wrong to think that he was an anarchist, an outlaw: This he had no wish to be. And incidentally we must also remember that Christians in general and theologians in particular have all too often seen Jesus only in the light of the Pauline controversies with the Jews. But it is different when you now ask me where the Synoptic Jesus—that is, the Jesus of the first three Gospels—stood with regard to the law.

First of all, in regard to the oral tradition, what you call *Halakhah* (you have made a distinction here, and not without reason), there are three things which cannot be disputed. Firstly, he thought very little of the regulations for cultic purity. Secondly, he did not think much of the fasting rules. And, thirdly, he attached little importance to the Sabbath prescriptions. All of which even today remain inviolable for the orthodox Jew.

And when he goes against oral tradition, against what we in a good Catholic sense also call tradition—in practice, insofar as his disciples simply do not keep to it—he has naturally indirectly impugned the Torah itself, the written law of Moses. For this law itself prescribed what must be observed with regard to pure and impure foods. How the Sabbath was to be kept was also prescribed in the Torah itself, in the sacred law of God. And if you then ask me which actions of Jesus are directly opposed to the Mosaic law, I think I must point to the following examples of a lack of agreement with that law: the prohibition of divorce, which was permitted according to the law of Moses; the prohibition of oaths, which were likewise permitted by the law; also the prohibition of reprisals; finally and especially the precept of love of enemies.

At every turn then he acts in a way that was not foreseen in the Old Testament. And it must be admitted, I think, that it is not so easy to turn him into a liberal Jew as, for instance, your coreligionist and theological colleague David Flusser—whom I greatly respect—has done in his book on Jesus. If he had been merely a liberal Jew, he would have had no more difficulties than, for instance, the liberal rabbi Hillel.

PINCHAS LAPIDE: I think the alternative is wrongly stated, if you put it in this way: Was Jesus for or against the Torah? Jesus was more for the Torah than a large part of the supposed or sham Pharisees. I shall try to explain this. Your example, the prohibition of divorce, was one of the great grounds for dispute between the two classical Pharisee schools of Hillel and Shammai. And, in the two different sayings of Jesus which have come down to us—according to Mark and Matthew he says two different things on divorce—it is interesting to see that according to Mark he adopts Hillel's position and according to Matthew Shammai's position: both schools of the Pharisees who dispute legitimately and fraternally about the interpretation of one and the same saying of the Bible. As the Talmud so democratically expresses it in such cases, without deciding the question, it notes at the end of the discussion: "Both the one and the other are words of the living God."

HANS KÜNG: We certainly cannot investigate every example here. But it might perhaps be a good thing to consider one of them more closely. For the question of divorce is also of current interest. Does it not seem to you that Jesus, particularly on the question of divorce, really did not bother at all about the scholastic disputes of theologians and jurists? In particular, he did not settle the question disputed between Hillel and Shammai: I agree with you on this matter. He just did not decide what exactly the grounds had to be or could be for a divorce or a certificate of divorce, as it was then called, which had to be drawn up by the husband. He was concerned with something much more fundamental.

It seems to me that an important point finds expression here. He simply did not want to give any individual solutions. But he said that marriage should never be dissolved and meant by this that he had behind him, not indeed the law of Moses, but certainly the Old Testament as a whole and in particular the story of creation, and that in this light these secondary questions ought to be discussed. Basically —and this is important for the modern state of the question—it was a question of protection for the woman, who had no legal opportunities at all and was completely underrated, since the husband could dismiss her entirely one-sidedly.

In this sense then, it seems to me that in all these legal questions Jesus was concerned with man's well-being: whether they refer to divorce, to the Sabbath, or to the rules of purification. And, I think, the question is whether I rightly understand Jesus here when I say: He was not concerned simply with the law and the fulfilling of the law, but essentially with what is the supreme norm, the will of God, that the will of God is the total well-being (salvation) of men. For that reason there may occasionally be an infringement of the Sabbath, an infringement of the food regulations, an infringement also of the rules for divorce. In brief, precepts exist for men and not men for precepts.

PINCHAS LAPIDE: Dr. Küng, which Jesus do you want? The Jesus who says in one of the Gospels, "There is absolutely no divorce," or the Jesus who says in another Gospel, on the same question, "except in the case of fornication?" You must make up your mind, my friend.

HANS KÜNG: My dear friend, I am glad to decide for Mark's version. As all biblical scholars say today, precisely in the oldest Gospel, that of Mark, it is laid down without any exception: You shall not have any divorce, you belong to each other. And Matthew's addition, "except in the case of fornication," is evidently meant to modify the original statement since people are now suddenly beginning to make a law out of what Jesus understood as an appeal, a call, and to say:

Yes, but now we must consider whether perhaps an exception ought to be made in the event of adultery by the other party.

May I only say this, in order not to be misunderstood today and by this audience: I think, for this very reason, that even today we cannot deduce from this text how we have to proceed in cases where there has in fact been a divorce, where the bond has been dissolved. I think that here too we cannot turn Jesus' words into a law in the opposite sense and claim that no reconciliation with the Church is possible if someone has obtained a divorce and married again. I think then that Jesus' words amounted and still amount to a great appeal, an invitation, as a father invites his son: This is not done, it is simply not done. But it does not mean that this is a rigid law in the sense that if the son nevertheless does this thing, the father throws him out of the house once and for all.

PINCHAS LAPIDE: Here I must tell you quite clearly, if you prefer the Marcan Jesus on divorce, that he was not an advocate of women's rights and that he stood quite squarely for the school of Shammai, even to the point of Essenism, and it can be proved that he was not original in this respect. But I will tell you something, Professor Küng, which will perhaps make me as unpopular in Jerusalem as you are possibly in Rome. There were dozens of rabbis before Jesus and after him who took the liberty of changing the words of the Torah— that is, words of divine instruction—in three ways: modifying, reinterpreting, or sharpening.

We have a wonderful Jesus-pericope in the Talmud, which has not —God knows why—up to now been adequately studied and interpreted, where Jesus does precisely the same. He deals with the question, which sounds very plebeian but was so much more realistic: May a prostitute's pay be used for the temple tax? That is, may the wages of sin be applied to a sacred purpose? And he gives a religiolegal judgment in a disputed question which changes a Torah saying in virtue of a prophet's saying. It is exactly the same with alleged infringements of the Sabbath law. The Sabbath, which is six times "canonized," declared holy, in the Bible, according to the rabbis even from Maccabean times, that is about a hundred and eighty years before Jesus, can be broken in two cases: In one it even *must* be broken, particularly when it is a question of the sanctity of human life. Jesus' saying, "You are lords of the Sabbath and the Sabbath is not lord of you," is handed down in almost the same words in the Talmud. I am sorry to detract from the originality of Jesus in this respect, but there it is. And the second case, where infringement of the Sabbath becomes a precept—not only permitted, but obligatory—is that of self-defense. If Israel is attacked—as it was, for instance, on the Sabbath of the Day of Atonement in 1973—to take up arms and to engage in all forms of military activity on the Sabbath is not only permitted but quite clearly obligatory. And so it happened also in all Israel. In this sense Jesus reinterpreted some statutes. For me this makes him so much the more rabbinical and not—God forbid—anti-Torah in his mentality as some of your writers on Christology wanted him to be.

HANS KÜNG: I would not dispute the existence of parallels with rabbis of earlier times; in this respect some things have been investigated and I think that more might well be found. You know that the important thing is not that you find one parallel or another or that here too someone once said something similar. I think that what is important for us is just this: in the light of what assumptions these things—for instance, on the Sabbath—are said, with what results, with what radicalness, and finally with what effects on history. None of these rabbis quoted by you ever had such difficulties as Jesus of Nazareth with the Jewish establishment. And none of them was liquidated, as he was, because of all that is recorded in the Synoptic Gospels. And in this sense neither is there anyone who so became the destiny of both the Jewish and also the Christian people as this one did. Hence my very direct question: Why, do you think, Jesus of Nazareth was liquidated at that time? And, if the sources are correct, why was he almost bound to be liquidated?

PINCHAS LAPIDE: I think that is fairly clear. I want to say just one last word on Jesus and the Torah: on his attitude to all the commandments, from the least to the greatest. He gives a wonderful example of both the slightest, that is, the tithe of dill and of mint—there is certainly nothing smaller—and of the greatest commandments, that is, twofold love—love of neighbor and love of God. On both he says all that he has to say in a splendid sentence in Matthew 23:23: "You ought to do the one without neglecting the other." No rabbi whom I know could have put it better.

Now on the death of Jesus: This I find terrible. I would in fact have wanted much more of his teaching than that of the brief thirty-three years which he was permitted to spend on earth. First of all, he never committed blasphemy: not according to any of the Synoptics,

nor according to John, in the clear, literal descriptions of the so-
called trial before the Sanhedrin. I'm sorry, but you must accept this.
In the Mishnah there is an extensive treatise on blasphemy and it is
there stated to a hair's breadth what blasphemy means according to
Jewish law and what it does not. And, according to these quite precise definitions, Jesus in no way committed blasphemy either before
the Sanhedrin or anywhere else in the Gospels: So Caiaphas' tearing
his robes remains an enigma for me. There was no occasion for him
to tear his clothes nor had he any right to plead here for a religiolegal condemnation.

Something else happened. And this is so clear in the Latin above
the cross that it is impossible to miss: that is, INRI. *Jesu Nazarenus
rex Judaeorum* is a purely political matter and—as you must admit
—it was this that interested Pontius Pilate, while the quibbling and
hairsplitting about the Mosaic laws left him absolutely cold. As
Roman "Gauleiter" he was no more interested in religious laws than
Hitler was in the Talmud. But rebellion against the Empire was his
affair, and jurisdiction in such matters belonged to him alone. When
he wrote INRI above the cross, he was acting in accordance with the
regulations of the *Lex Julia Majestatis,* which we know very well
from Roman sources. So this Jesus was condemned by Pilate for attempted rebellion or for assuming the title of king. I have not the
slightest difficulty in seeing that *Mashiah Israel*—that is, the Messiah
of Israel—as many Jews in Israel hailed him, meant for the Romans
in Jerusalem in A.D. 30 precisely what "King of the Irish" in Dublin
in 1920 would have meant to the English governor: a summons to
rebellion and the overthrow of the alien yoke.

HANS KÜNG: There are two points here—the question of blasphemy
and the political question—and I would like to say something on
both. *Firstly,* on the question of blasphemy, I would agree with you
that what on a naive reading of the Bible very often seems to be the
essential point—that is, blasphemy, that he made himself out to be
God's Son—was later interpreted in this sense by the community. I
do not think—and today all serious New Testament scholars would
agree—that he simply made himself out to be God or that he quite
formally described himself as Son of God. In the three older Gospels
Jesus himself appears to be very reserved in regard to all titles. But
there was surely something in the background to explain why
Caiaphas tore his robe or at any rate why the leading circles were interested in his liquidation.

Two things, it seems to me, played a part here. The one, to which I have already alluded, was that this attitude to the law seemed to them unacceptable: that it was bound to undermine the entire social order if it were said that every law and every precept existed for the sake of men and not vice versa; if a different attitude were adopted to Samaritans, to enemies as a whole; above all, if someone boldly gave a personal assurance of forgiveness of sin here and now. It is clear from the Gospels that this attitude to the law was one factor. The second obviously related to worship and the temple. This Jesus —and presumably others also—thought that the temple was not eternal and that worship of God was secondary to service to man. According to the Gospels, then, these are the real reasons why he was condemned.

Secondly, a very brief word on the political question. I do not think that this played such a dominant part, at any rate for the Jewish authorities who condemned him. I agree with you wholly and entirely that the question of a possible rebellion could have been the main point for the Roman governor or—as you aptly call him— "Gauleiter." I think too that he was actually condemned as a political rebel by the Roman occupying power. But on the other hand it is certain that he did not himself use precisely the title which you mention, that he did not himself assume in particular the title of Messiah; that presumably—as again scholars today agree—he did not use any title, except perhaps "Son of man," which was deliberately ambiguous and provided no clear information. It would therefore be wrong to think that someone came and said, "I am the Messiah," and thus started a dangerous revolutionary movement.

As to his political attitude, he dissociated himself quite definitely from the revolutionary movement of the Zealots; he rejected the use of force; it would be possible—you could certainly do it, and I could but will not—to draw up a whole list of differences which separated him from the political revolts of his time. His invitation to nonviolence offered in different forms decisively shows that the revolutionaries would have liked to make him their ringleader, but that he himself could not accept this. In this sense, I think, the question of the cause of death ought therefore to be seen, not only in political but properly in religious terms.

PINCHAS LAPIDE: Three points on this, Dr. Küng. If someone rides into Jerusalem on a messianic animal—and there is no doubt that the donkey of Bethany was such—then all Israel would see in it an

allusion to Zechariah 9:9. If, moreover, that person is welcomed
joyously with cries of "Hosanna" by thousands, he has no need to
declare himself the Messiah. All this is so clear and the crowds are
already so unanimous, particularly at the time of the feast, that is,
the Passover Feast, the classical point of time of redemption in
Jerusalem. This festal mood, this entry, the cries of "Hosanna," and
a dozen other hints and allusions, which I will spare you here, point
so directly to a messianity of Jesus that they must have been more
than sufficient for Pilate.

I agree with you however that Jesus was undoubtedly a thorn in
the flesh for many Sadducees. A man who insisted so clearly on the
priority of ethics over worship, over the monopoly of those Sadducees of the temple hierarchy, for them was bound to be at least a
disturber of the peace if not worse. I am therefore certain that some
of the temple rulers had a part in his condemnation. But the fact that
Jews in the shape of a couple of Sadducees helped to get him condemned by Pilate no more diminishes Roman culpability for his
death than, we might say, the fact that a Dutchman betrayed Anne
Frank and her family to the Gestapo: the same Gestapo which had
Anne Frank together with her whole family cremated in Auschwitz.
The Dutchman is not guilty of these deaths, although he helped to be-
tray them; the Sadducees did not bring him to the cross, although
they helped to bring about his condemnation. Pilate was the only one
who had the power to impose the death penalty.

And if, as you say, Jesus put ethics before worship, he was in good
company. Centuries before his time, both Isaiah and also Amos and
Malachi said the same thing in words which remain immortal. "I do
not want your sacrifices," they said, speaking in the name of God; "I
am angered by your sacrifices. Let justice prevail and welcome the
orphans and widows, and only then—says the Lord—bring me your
offerings." Jesus then was neither alone nor original in his emphasis
on the priority of ethics.

HANS KÜNG: There is, of course, a great deal that I could say here,
but I completely agree with you that the Roman guilt should in no
way be minimized. The evangelists themselves tend—understandably
—to exonerate the Roman political authority under which they had
to live. But I think we should see both sides. The very fact that Jesus
rode into Jerusalem on a donkey shows that he did not want to enter
on a white horse, the mount of a radiant victor, or even like an em-
peror or one of the kings of Israel: With the donkey there is linked a

very different symbolism. The problem cannot be solved in the light only of these things. But I do not think we need be obsessed with them. Here at any rate we have reached a point at which we ought to continue our discussion, where Christians and Jews as a whole ought to continue discussion today: Where did the real controversy lie at the time and why was he killed? If that were a little clearer, I think we would come closer without more ado.

WALTER STROLZ: Anyone who has followed this discussion will be wondering what it is that really distinguishes Christianity from Judaism, when we remember—Rabbi Lapide—what you have said on Jesus' Jewish conception of the Torah. How could an independent line of a Christian faith continue throughout two thousand years if the affinity with Judaism is infinitely greater than the distinguishing features? Or, to state the question in another way, have we still not even approached the really distinctive feature, the scandal of Christian faith?

HANS KÜNG: This undoubtedly is the decisive thing: What is it on the whole that distinguishes Christians from Jews, that has distinguished them from the very beginning? I would answer this quite tersely: The distinguishing feature is that Jesus as the Christ is rejected by the Jews and recognized by the Christians. In this respect the title is not important. Christ means Messiah, but people also gave him other titles, from Son of man in the highest sense to Son of God. The titles are not decisive. But this much is clear: For Christians this Jesus of Nazareth is the authoritative standard and he is not only—as Karl Jaspers says—one of the archetypal human beings (*massgebende Menschen*), but the archetype properly so-called. This would be the real difference. For a Jew, if I understand it rightly, now as before, the law is the authoritative standard and not this Jesus of Nazareth.

PINCHAS LAPIDE: Dr. Küng, I would express it in two words: Christianity is a "who" religion; Judaism is a "what" religion. Or, if you want it in another way, Judaism is a redemption religion while Christianity is a redeemer religion. For you the redeemer, the king, is important; for us the kingdom. We Jews know—under God—a heavenly kingdom even without the savior-king, but we do not know any savior-king without a kingdom already here. Television and the press however confirm the fact every day with appalling clarity that this world is unredeemed. But, as far as the good news is concerned, you

Christians have two reasons to be grateful to us: First, because of
our fidelity to Jesus; for it is due solely to Jewish fidelity to Jesus that
there was a Paul and a primitive Church, all called into life and
founded by pure, full Jews. And, secondly, you have reason to be
grateful to us on account of our later "infidelity." For if Paul's initial
mission to the Jews had not been a failure, as is so clearly shown in
the Acts of the Apostles, he would perhaps not have gone to the Gentiles. It was only then that he began to bring the good news to the
Gentiles and thus made possible the emergence of a Gentile Christianity. You should then thank us for our fidelity, which found its expression in Paul and in the primitive Church, and for our corresponding infidelity, which permitted you to become Christians.

HANS KÜNG: I do not really want to decide to what extent we have
to be grateful. I would prefer to see gratitude elsewhere. In any case
it is not precisely Paul who should be cited here, since he is, of
course, the principal witness to the fact that it is the profession of
faith in Jesus as the Christ which divides us. For him this Christ
Jesus has actually taken the place of the law. And in this sense I find
very illuminating what you say about the difference between a "who"
and a "what" religion. I think too that in this respect there is a
different emphasis in Christianity. This is involved in the very name.
"Christian" comes from "Christ"; it comes from this Jesus, the
Christ. The emphasis therefore is on the person, there is no doubt
about this.

   Naturally this is not something we would want to play off against
each other. Redeemer and redemption go together, as king and kingdom go together. We would also agree with you in this decisive argument which is continually raised by Jews against the Christian message: that redemption in the sense of consummation is not yet truly
present; that the kingdom in which every tear will be wiped away
from men's eyes, where suffering, pain, and death will have disappeared, is not yet truly here. In this sense it is Jesus Christ who announced this kingdom.

   For us, of course, a point is involved here which certainly should
not be passed over: namely, that Jesus himself has already reached
what is understood as the kingdom of God. As Christians, we believe
that he is basically the brief recapitulation or—if you prefer—the
formula, so to speak, of the kingdom of God: for in him in effect all
that he expected in the immediate future—that is, the kingdom of
God—was fulfilled. It would then be very interesting to hear from

you at least briefly what you really think of the conviction we share with the first Christian community that the one who ended on the gallows crying out his forsakenness by God and men was nevertheless taken up into the glory of God; that he did not simply remain in death, that his death is not the end of everything; in a word, that he lives with God and through God. What do you think of the problem of the "resurrection" (a somewhat ambiguous term) of Jesus from the dead?

PINCHAS LAPIDE: Up to a short time ago I thought that anything like a self-abasement of God—kenosis—and incarnation in the Christian sense were alien to Judaism. To my astonishment, I have learned in the meantime that there were germinal traces of both ideas among marginal groups in Judaism as early as the first century before Christ and still more in the first and second Christian centuries, so that even these things entered later Christianity not from Hellenism but in fact from certain Jewish circles. With the utmost seriousness, as an orthodox Jew, I must say that I cannot accept what you call resurrection, kenosis, and apocatastasis, since this is not suggested by our Jewish experience of God. But neither can I deny it, for who am I as a devout Jew to define a priori God's saving action? To *define* means to assign limits, and this, from a Jewish standpoint, would be blasphemous. Can I prescribe something to God in the way that your medieval theologians attempted to imprison him—the Lord of the world—within a system? Can he and his unsearchable ways be squeezed onto a piece of paper, into a book, or into any kind of theological system? That would be absurd. *I don't know.* That is all I can say, but—unlike the Jewish-Christian controversialists of the last eighteen hundred years, when people turned more and more blatantly from opponents into enemies—I can answer today with a biblical and humble "I do not know." I would change the angle of vision of our controversy, which has now lasted almost nineteen centuries, from 180 degrees—that is, from a Christian "Yes" in confrontation with a Jewish "No"—to one, if you want, of 90 degrees—that is, to a Christian "Yes" and a modest Jewish "I do not know."

HANS KÜNG: I must admit that I am very impressed by your public admission at any rate or your not knowing. Incidentally, as a Christian, I would also say—and this perhaps may be a little easier for a Jew to understand—that those of our people who thought they could prove Jesus' resurrection were certainly mistaken. The attempt has

constantly been made simply to produce from the Gospel testimonies
—as, for example, the Easter stories, which are in a very legendary
style—a historical proof for you which Jews would have to accept. I
do not think it can be proved in this way.

What is possible—and this I think might perhaps bring us a little
closer—is something which seems to me quite in the spirit of the Old
Testament: simply to trust, to trust unswervingly that Jesus is living.
That God, therefore, who for Israel is in fact the Creator of the
world, is also its completer. That God, who according to the Israelite
conception has the first word, will also have the last word. That the
faith and trust of the first Christian community are therefore justified
and remain also authoritative for us. And that God then has basically
given his "Yes" also and in particular for Jesus, that for this reason
Jesus did not remain in death but in fact is living with God. He lives
on, we believe, as a hope not only for ourselves but for all men,
Christians and Jews. We believe that death does not mean the end of
everything but that our death too belongs to God; that we, therefore,
do not die—if you like to put it this way—from death into nothingness, but into that encompassing, greatest, last and first, most real reality which we call God.

PINCHAS LAPIDE: Professor Küng, what unites us is everything that
can be known and investigated with the tools of scholarship about
Jesus. What divide us are the things that divide not only Jews from
Christians but also knowledge from faith. One thing I know for certain: that faith in this Christ has given millions of Christians a better
life and an easier death, and I would be the last to disturb their faith
even if I could. Anyway I can't. What I can and will say is this: You
are waiting for the parousia; with you too the fullness of redemption
is still in the fuure; I await its coming, but the second coming is also
a coming. If the Messiah comes and then turns out to be Jesus of
Nazareth, I would say that I do not know of any Jew in this world
who would have anything against it.

Thus a legitimate awaiting his advent or second coming—and the
distinction here is really secondary—not only would be our common
expectation of salvation but in the meantime would enable both of us
to concentrate on what can be known. And here the thirty-three
earthly years of Jesus are a legitimate field of research for both of us.
We should leave our faith to God, since neither of us can talk the
other into it. We are living, thank God, in a religious pluralism. God

alone knows, of all the ways which lead to him, which is the shortest and best. I have no desire to assume papal authority to decide which of us believes better, more prudently, or more wisely.

HANS KÜNG: You have touched on a very fundamental point, and theoretically there is little more to be said on the subject. You said that faith in Jesus Christ had enabled countless Christians to lead a better life. This, I think, has all too often been forgotten in Christendom: that with Jesus it is not simply a question of a Christology, a doctrine, a Logos of Christ, but a question of following Christ. The whole history of relations between Christians and Jews would have taken a different course if Christians as practical disciples of Christ had made a better attempt to follow him instead of merely disputing theoretically with Jews how Christ is to be understood and how God is to be understood.

The decisive thing however is to attempt to live this message, which carries with it so many Jewish elements, which perhaps finds its most profound expression in the summing up of the law as it appears already in the book of Exodus: to love God with all our heart and our neighbor as ourselves I think, if we Christians had been more concerned with practice, we would have gotten further also in the dialogue. Then the situation in regard to these lofty teachings would be fundamentally different from what it is now, after always speaking mainly about lofty teachings and largely neglecting practical discipleship. What is credible is only *being* a Christian and not simply any kind of doctrine held by Christians.

PINCHAS LAPIDE: In a word, after living and praying *against one another* for nearly two thousand years, let us two study *with one another* and discover the earthly Jesus from below—as you say—and let us then see where God will further guide us both.

Translated by EDWARD QUINN

III. Catholics and Protestants

1. An Ecumenical Inventory

We hear complaints in the churches today that an increasing number of Christians are not at ease in any of the Christian churches and tend to form a kind of "third denomination," without attachment to a church. But how are we to cope with this ecclesial "homelessness" if the churches themselves are not becoming more impartial, more flexible, more hospitable also toward each other? For most people today the denominational differences arising from the Reformation have become completely irrelevant. Formerly Catholics knew Protestants only from hearsay and vice versa, while now the members of different denominations are in more or less close contact with one another. Under these circumstances many Christians ascribe the maintenance of the schism to unenlightened, inflexible ecclesiastics and their theologians intent on retaining power. Are they completely wrong in this opinion?

Certainly we cannot ignore *what has hitherto been achieved*. A survey of the ecumenical movement provides scarcely a hint of the labor, tenacity, hope against hope, which were necessary for decades in order merely to get the World Council of Churches established (1948). From a survey of Catholic ecumenism also we can only surmise what efforts and personal sacrifice it cost a few Catholic lay people and theologians, undaunted by the antiecumenical attitude of the popes up to Pius XII, to prepare for the breakthrough of the Catholic Church to ecumenicity under John XXIII and the Second Vatican Council (1962–65).

It is due to all these untiring efforts—against the background of cruel nationalistic experiences of "Christian" peoples in two World Wars—that relations between the churches claiming to follow Jesus Christ have been turned into something positive. And if we look even further back, to the Reformation period, we can see how much the Catholic view of Martin Luther's personality has changed: We can also note the change of temper in Catholic and Protestant "controversial theology": the early polemic gave way to attempts to bring out the differences in the official teaching of the denominations, with the result that subjective polemics were overcome and an "ecumenical" theology emerged. Which means that the churches and their theologies have traveled a long way from denunciation and inquisition to communication and discussion, from denominational coexistence to ecumenical co-operation.

It is true that the Catholic Church in particular has not yet joined the World Council of Churches and presents special difficulties for an ecumenical agreement because of its tradition, teaching, and organization (and especially the primacy and infallibility of the pope). But the fact cannot be overlooked that, in comparison with the post-Tridentine, Counter-Reformation Church—despite all compromises —the basic trend of the Second Vatican Council amounted to a turn of 180 degrees in the direction of ecumenicity. Despite all the remaining unresolved problems (birth control, divorce, ministry, mixed marriages, celibacy, primacy, and infallibility), the concrete *positive results* must not be underestimated. They also provoke *further questions*—to be at least briefly indicated here—to the other churches.

1. Since the Second Vatican Council, what has changed *for Christendom as a whole?*
    a. The Catholic *share of guilt* for the schism is now recognized. At the same time the necessity of continual *reform* is accepted: *Ecclesia semper reformanda*—continual renewal of our own Church in life and teaching according to the gospel. But the further question arises: May the other churches then regard themselves as in no need of reform (Orthodox Church) or even as already reformed (Lutheran and Calvinist churches), or are they also still to be reformed?
    b. The other Christian communities are *recognized as churches*. In all churches there is a common Christian basis which is perhaps more important than everything that divides them. But again the question arises: Ought there not to be a more intense effort to find the common Christian basis and "substance" also in the other churches?
    c. An *ecumenical attitude* is required from the whole Church. There must be an inward conversion of Catholics themselves, a

growth of mutual understanding between the churches and a readiness to learn by dialogue, a recognition of the faith, the baptism, the values of other Christians, finally a theology and church history worked out in an ecumenical spirit. But there is a further question: Will the other churches then, for their part, also recognize and realize the numerous Catholic concerns in theology, liturgy, and church structures?

d. *Co-operation* with other Christians is to be promoted in every way. There must be practical collaboration in the whole social field, but also prayer together and increasingly a united worshiping community—especially in the liturgy of the word—and finally discussion between theologians of equal standing. Here, too, a further question must be faced: Ought not the other churches also to develop more strongly a readiness to co-operate?

2. What has changed in regard to the *churches of the Reformation* since the Second Vatican Council? A whole series of concerns which were central to the Reformers have been accepted at least in principle by the Catholic Church.

a. *A new appreciation of the Bible:* (i) In worship: Proclamation, prayer, and hymns should all bear the imprint of a biblical spirit; a new and more varied cycle of Scripture readings covering a number of years has been produced. (ii) In the life of the Church as a whole: Instead of insistence on the Latin Vulgate translation there is now a demand for modern translations of the Bible from the original text; instead of the former prohibition of Bible reading by the laity there are now repeated invitations to read the Bible frequently. (iii) In theology: The Church's magisterium is not above God's word but exists to serve the latter; it is no longer the universal teaching of the Church that revealed truth is contained "partly" in Scripture and "partly" in tradition; the study of Scripture must be the "soul" of theology (and of catechetics), the justification of the historical-critical interpretation of Scripture is recognized, the inerrancy of Scripture is claimed not for statements on natural science but only for truths of salvation.

b. *Genuine people's worship:* the realization of the concerns of the Reformers can be seen in a number of examples: (i) As against the former clerical liturgy, there is a service involving the whole priestly people through an intelligible structure and active participation of the whole congregation in common prayer, singing and meal. (ii) As against the former proclamation in the alien Latin language, there is a new attention to the word of God proclaimed in the vernacular. (iii) As against the standardized, uniform Roman liturgy, there is adaptation to the different nations; national episcopates with shared competence instead of the formerly exclusive papal competence. (iv) As against the former proliferation and concealment, there is now simplification and concentration on essentials: revision of all rites and thus a greater similarity between the Mass and the last supper of Jesus. (v) There is reform also of the liturgy of the sacraments, of the church year, of the breviary. (vi) Included in all this is a positive settlement of classical points of controversy (vernacular and the chalice for the laity are likewise permitted in principle).

c. *Revaluation of the laity:* Direct access of the laity to the Scriptures and the realization of the people's worship are themselves an important fulfillment of this third concern of the Reformers. In addition, there are numerous theological publications on the importance of the laity in the Church, with an implicit criticism of clericalism; every bishop is expected to set up a pastoral council consisting of priests and lay people.

d. *Adaptation of the Church to the nations:* As against a centralized system, the importance of the local churches and the particular churches (dioceses, nations) is stressed; national and continental conferences of bishops are to promote practical decentralization; the Roman Curia itself is to be internationalized.

e. *Reform of popular piety:* There has been a reform of fasting regulations, of indulgences and devotional practices. Restrictions have been imposed on the excesses of Marian devotion (the Second Vatican Council set up clear limits in this respect by rejecting a separate document on Mary); nor was any additional Marian dogma promulgated.

This largely completed realization of the concerns of the Reformers again raises further questions. Should not the Protestant churches now make it their business to approach Catholics effectively with more self-critical understanding? To put it quite concretely:

appreciation of the Bible, certainly: but where does Protestantism stand in regard to its neglect of the common tradition of the early Church and of the Middle Ages?

genuine liturgy of the word and people's worship, certainly: but what of the celebration of the eucharist, thrust into the background or even practically excluded in Protestant churches?

revaluation of the laity, certainly: but what of the importance of ordination and the Church's ministry (also beyond the limits of a particular region)?
adaptation to the nations, certainly: but what of the international
and universal character of the Church, so often put in question by
Protestant provincialism?
reform of popular piety, certainly: but what of the closeness of the
Church and its worship to the people, often imperiled by Protestant
intellectualism?

3. What has changed in regard to the *Eastern churches,* which have
often been regarded as merely an appendage of the Latin Church?
Since Vatican II the churches of the East have been expressly recognized as enjoying equal rights with those of the West. Rebaptism is
not required of Orthodox Christians who become Catholics, nor are
Orthodox priests expected to be reordained, and celibacy is not imposed on them. If they want to do so, Orthdox Christians may receive the sacraments in Catholic churches; on the other hand, if no
Catholic priest is available, Catholics may receive the sacraments in
Orthodox churches. Mixed marriages between Catholics and Orthodox are valid, even if they are not contracted in Catholic churches.
Ought not all these things to hold also with reference to the Protestant churches? Immediately before the close of the council there took
place simultaneously in Rome and Constantinople the solemn revo-
cation of the mutual excommunication of 1054, which had inaugu-
rated the schism between East and West, lasting almost a thousand
years. But does not this very act require both sides to face its consequences, particularly in regard to the eucharistic community? The
Orthodox Churches remained far too static, rigidly holding to the position not of the primitive Church but of the Byzantine centuries.
Ought not they also to have roused themselves to a serious reform of
their liturgy, theology, and church structures? But on the other hand
the Catholic Church rigidly upheld the primacy of jurisdiction and
papal infallibility in its relations with the Orthodox churches. Ought
we not honestly to re-examine both questions in the light of the New
Testament and the common early church tradition, instead of refus-
ing to discuss these points of doctrine?

    In fact, as even Pope Paul VI has admitted, the *papacy* with its ab-
solute claim is the main difficulty in the way of ecumenical agreement. But is an agreement on this subject possible at all? Yes, if (a)

the papal *primacy* is understood less as a primacy of honor or jurisdiction and more as a pastoral primacy in the service of the unity of
the Church as a whole; (b) papal infallibility is understood as the
function of witnessing and proclaiming in the service of the "infallibility" or, better, "indefectibility"—that is, of the indestructibility—
of the Church in truth, despite all errors in detail.

The rest of the doctrinal differences with reference to Scripture
and tradition, grace and justification, Church and sacraments may be
regarded as largely settled in theological terms. The situation can be
summed up briefly and systematically. Today the primacy of *Scripture* as the original Christian testimony (normative norm) prior to
all later *tradition* is acknowledged also by Catholic theology and, on
the other hand, the importance of postbiblical tradition (regulated
norm) is admitted at least in principle by Protestant theology.
Justification in virtue of faith alone is affirmed by Catholic theologians, just as the necessity of works or deeds of love is affirmed by
Protestant theologians.

Fortunately, much more has happened among the ordinary people
in the churches. Mutual understanding today in a large number of
Catholic, Protestant, and Orthodox congregations has increased to
an extent formerly inconceivable. There is intercommunion already
among many groups. This actually living ecumenicity at the base is
more important for the future than all theological controversies and
all finely spun ecclesiastical diplomacy. Nevertheless, a more inten-
sive support for ecumenical efforts must be expected from the leadership of the churches, particularly in regard to urgent *ecumenical im-
peratives* such as (a) reform and mutual recognition of church
ministries, (b) common liturgy of the word and open communion,
(c) common building and common use of churches and other structures, (d) common fulfillment of service to society, (e) increasing
integration of theological faculties and religious instruction, (f)
drawing up of concrete plans for union on the part of church leaders
at national and universal levels.

Ecumenicity is more than mere activism in reform. It can be found
and realized only if all the churches concentrate afresh on the one
Christian tradition, on the gospel of Jesus Christ himself. Only in
that light can denominational fears and uncertainties be reduced, ideological fanaticism and bitter prejudice be overcome, the economic,
political, cultural entanglements with a particular society, social stra-
tum, class, race, or state concealed behind theological differences be

discerned, and an advance be made toward a new freedom. This of course means that there can be no ecumenical agreement without renewal in the Church, but also no renewal in the Church without ecumenical agreement.

But what then is "Catholic" and what is "Protestant"? In the future the differences will continue to find expression only in diverse traditional *basic attitudes* which have developed from the time of the Reformation but can be integrated today into a true ecumenicity.

a. Who is *Catholic?* Someone who attaches special importance to the Catholic—that is, *entire,* universal, all-encompassing, total— Church. In the concrete, to the *continuity* of faith in time and the community of faith in space, maintained in all disruptions.

b. Who is *Protestant?* Someone who attaches special importance in all traditions, doctrines, and practices of the Church to constant, critical recourse to the gospel (Scripture) and to constant, practical *reform* according to the norm of the gospel.

c. But from all this it is clear that "Catholic" and "Protestant" basic attitudes, correctly understood, are by no means mutually exclusive. Today even the "born" Catholic can be truly Protestant and the "born" Protestant truly Catholic in his mentality, so that even now in the whole world there are innumerable Christians who— despite the obstructions of the churches' machinery—do in fact realize a genuine ecumenicity finding its center in the light of the gospel. Being truly Christian today means being an *ecumenical Christian.*

Such an ecumenical Church of the future certainly must not dissolve into disparate, unorganized groups. But, despite the fact that it must also have an institutional character, it would not be a single party organization, an absolutist religious Roman Empire. This ecumenical Church of the future would be marked by more truthfulness, freedom, humanity, by more broad-mindedness, tolerance, and magnanimity, more Christian self-confidence, supreme composure, and courage to think and to decide. Such a Church would not always be behind the times but as far as possible ahead of them. It might be the avant-garde of a better humanity.

Translated by EDWARD QUINN

2. What Is the Essence of Apostolic Succession?

The concept of apostolic succession suffers from undue clerical and juridical constriction. We do not breathe the free air of the Bible and this paralyzes our ecumenism. New life can be breathed into it only by a return to Scripture. How this can be done is summarized here in a few theses which I have dealt with more in detail elsewhere.[1]

1. Basic is the point that the *whole Church* and *every individual member* share in this apostolic succession: The Church as a whole is committed to obedience to the Apostles as the original witnesses and the original messengers. In the *negative* sense this means that the concept suffers from a clerical narrowing down if this apostolic succession is seen exclusively as a succession of ecclesiastical functions. In the *positive* sense it means that the whole Church is involved. It is the Church as a whole that we believe in when we say "I believe in the apostolic Church." The Church as a whole is successor to the Apostles. And insofar as the Church is not an institutional apparatus but the community of the faithful, this means that every individual member of the Church stands in this apostolic succession. Every later generation remains bound to the word, the witness, and the service of the first apostolic generation. The Apostles are and remain the once-for-all and irreplaceable original witnesses, their witness the sole original witness, their mission the sole original mission. The whole Church is founded on the foundation of the Apostles (and the Prophets).

2. The apostolic succession of the Church as a whole and of every individual consists in this *essential cohesion with the Apostles,* to be put into practice constantly; it demands the constant accord with the apostolic *witness* (Scripture) and the constant rendering of the apostolic *service* (missionary extension in the world and the building up of the community). Apostolic succession is therefore primarily a succession in apostolic faith, apostolic service, and apostolic life. This means in the *negative* sense that it is a juridical narrowing of the concept to see apostolic succession primarily in a continuous chain of impositions of hands—as if such a chain of ordinations could supply by itself the apostolic spirit! In the *positive* sense it

means that the point of the succession lies in the constantly renewed daily loyalty to the Apostles. This means not fanaticism but sober obedience. The Apostles are dead. Any authority and power in the Church can only arise from obedience to the Lord of the Church and the Apostles. Apostolicity is at the same time a gift and a task. Both the Church as a whole and every individual member need to be in harmony with the apostolic witness: They can only hear the Lord and his message via this apostolic witness. In fact, sound *ecclesiastical* tradition can only be an interpretation, explanation, and application of the original *apostolic* tradition, contained in Scripture. And the Church cannot be true to this apostolic witness otherwise than through continuing the apostolic service in its many forms of proclamation, baptism, the communion in prayer and the eucharistic meal, the building up of the community, and service to the world.

3. Within the apostolic succession of the Church as a whole there is a special apostolic succession of the many *pastoral* services, through which the pastors, without being apostles themselves, continue the mission and function of the Apostles—namely, the founding and guiding of the Church. In the *negative* sense this means that apostolic succession becomes a mere abstraction if we divorce it from the historical reality. We must not only see the Church as a whole but also in the concrete reality of her many services which are not all equally important. In the *positive* sense it means that the pastors are not apostles but continue the mission and function of the Apostles by founding and leading the Church. They are not a governing class with a one-sided power to command. But there is a superposition and a subordination, determined by the kind of service.

4. Among the many charismatic gifts of leadership which continue the apostolic mission, the pastoral services of *presbyter* (pastor), *episkopos* (bishop), and *diakonos* (deacon), based on a particular function (imposition of hands), came to stand out with increasing prominence during the postapostolic age. This means in the *negative* sense that we make an undue presupposition when we draw a simple straight line of succession from the Apostles to the bishops. Apart from those charisms that appear freely and by their very nature cannot be brought under a system ("being the first," stewards, presidents, guides, etc.), it is equally impossible to systematize the services transmitted by imposition of hands (at least at that time), such as presbyters, *episkopoi,* deacons, etc., on the basis of the New Testament. The threefold order of functions mentioned by Ignatius of

Antioch has, no doubt, its roots in the original period but can not simply be identified as the whole original order and distribution of all the functions. It is the result of a very complex historical development. It is also impossible to trace the dividing line that separates these three functions among themselves, particularly in the case of the *episkopos* and the presbyter, on the basis of *dogmatic theology*. It means in the *positive* sense that the distinction between the various services is, on the one hand, a matter of factual development and, on the other, of pastoral expediency. Even if one wholly accepts the threefold division of the Church's function into presbyters, bishops, and deacons as a meaningful and practical development, one cannot treat such a juridical definition, which at most is the practical realization of *but one* possibility, as if it were a dogmatic necessity. The rich beginnings of a church order in the New Testament leave plenty of room for other possibilities in practice.

5. Pastoral service as a special kind of succession to the Apostles is surrounded in the Church by *other gifts* and services, particularly in those that have succeeded to the New Testament *prophets* and *teachers* who, in co-operation with the pastors, have their own original authority. This means in the *negative* sense that, through an unbiblical limitation, canalization, and monopolization of the free charism in the Church, there arises a kind of pastoral hierocracy when pastors feel that they alone possess the Spirit and so try to quench the Spirit in others. There is an un-Pauline absolutization of a function when an official considers himself to be apostle, prophet, and teacher all at once and so wants to grasp everything unto himself. In the *positive* sense it means that every individual stands in the line of apostolic succession according to the particular charism that has been bestowed on him. This succession is therefore not limited to the one line of pastoral services. There is also—and second in the order of St. Paul—the succession of the prophets in whom the Spirit expresses himself directly and who, in their awareness of their calling and responsibility, show the way, present and future, in a given situation of the Church. And, third in St. Paul's list, there is the succession of the teachers, the theologians who go to endless trouble in order to transmit and interpret in a genuine way the message of the past in the present situation of Church and world.

6. The *pastoral succession with imposition of hands* is neither automatic nor mechanical. It presupposes faith and demands a faith that is active in the apostolic spirit. It does not exclude the possibility

of failure and error and therefore needs to be tested by the community of the faithful. This means in the *negative* sense: Any isolated mechanism of succession of an official hierarchy which makes abstraction of the human condition and, by the same token, of the constantly necessary grace of God, of the constantly new demands on faith and life, cannot appeal to the New Testament. The power of the community, of the universal priesthood, cannot be simply derived from the pastoral service. That would be an unbiblical clericalization of the community, would separate the pastoral service from the universal priesthood and absolutize it in its succession. On the other hand, the power of the pastoral service also cannot be derived from the power of the community and the universal priesthood. This would be an unbiblical secularization of the community and reduce the pastoral function to the level of the universal priesthood. In the *positive* sense it means that cohesion *and* distinction of pastoral service and the community with all its special gifts and services are important. The special call to the *public service of the community as such* by the imposition of hands, the ordination, must be seen against the background of the universal priesthood. We must therefore distinguish between the "empowering" of every Christian and the special power of some individuals for the public service of the community as such. All Christians are empowered to proclaim the word, to witness to the faith in the Church and in the world; all are "sent." But only those called to be pastors (or commissioned by them) have the special power to preach in the assembly of the community. All Christians are empowered to promise forgiveness to the brother troubled by conscience. But only those called to be pastors have the special power to pronounce the words of reconciliation and absolution in the assembly of the community as such and thus apply it to the individual. All Christians are empowered to take part in the administration of baptism and the eucharistic meal. But only those called to be pastors have the special power to administer baptism publicly and to preside responsibly over the communal eucharist.

7. The apostolic succession of the pastors must take place in the communion of mutual service to Church and world. Admission to the apostolic succession in the pastoral line should normally take place according to the mind of the New Testament through a *co-operation of pastors and community,* a co-operation of as many different elements as possible. This means in the *negative* sense that it is a false view of ecclesiastical office to see obedience and subordination

as a one-way traffic. The ecclesiastical functions are there for the community and not the community for the functions. An absolutist government of the Church, at the level of the whole Church, the diocese, or the parish, is a contradiction of the gospel. In the *positive* sense it means that, because of the specific mission of the pastor to the community, the pastoral function already implies an authority. The pastor has his credentials from the beginning, and he is officially accepted as empowered to fulfill this public service for the community. Nevertheless, this does in no way deprive the community of its right to examine whether the pastor acts in truth according to this mission, according to the gospel. The specific power given to the pastor even requires that every day he obediently use this power anew. But in spite of all the legitimate relative autonomy of the pastor (bishop or priest), the appointment of pastors in the Church must come about basically through a co-operation of those who already are pastors and the community. And apart from their appointment, even when the pastors are entitled to a certain responsible autonomy in the guidance of the community because they need this in the exercise of their function, nevertheless, the community as the royal priesthood should have a voice in all the affairs of the community, and this can be done directly or through a representative body. This corresponds to the juridical principle, so often quoted in the Church's tradition: "What concerns all must be dealt with by all."

8. If we base ourselves on the Pauline, or the Gentile Christian, church order, we must leave room for *other ways of pastoral service and apostolic succession* of pastors. The church order based on the presbyter and the *episkopos,* which has as a matter of fact prevailed in the Church, must today, too, remain open in principle to all the possibilities that existed in the Church of the New Testament. This means in the *negative* sense that the institutional order, mainly determined by the Palestinian tradition, must not be absolutized. The present organization of the offices in the Church developed essentially in three stages: (a) Over against the prophets, teachers, and other charismatic functionaries, the episcopal line (including presbyters and *episkopoi*) prevailed as the dominant and finally exclusive leaders of the community. (b) Over against the plurality of bishops (presbyters and bishops) within a community this led to a monarchical episcopacy. (c) From being the presidents of the individual communities the bishops became presidents of ecclesiastical territories. This schematic sketch of the development cannot be ruled out a

priori as unjustified. Nevertheless a definite new order cannot be proved right simply by arguing from the existing situation nor from the possible misuse of charisms. It is justified rather by the decisive difference between the original phase and the time that came after, between the apostolic age of the foundation and the postapostolic age of building up and expansion. In the *positive* sense this means: an exposé of the Pauline church order can demonstrate that a charismatic order of the community is possible without a specific admission to a service (ordination), and that perchance Corinth knew of neither *episkopoi* nor presbyters nor any kind of ordination but only free and spontaneous charisms, apart from the Apostles. And yet, according to Paul, the church of Corinth was a community provided with all that was necessary, equipped with the proclamation of the word, baptism, eucharist, and all other services. On the other hand, there is at the same time enough evidence to show that these Pauline communities showed relatively soon that there were bishops and deacons, and, after Paul, ordained priests, so that the presbyteral and episcopal order became general in the Church. Nevertheless, the Church as it developed later cannot in principle exclude the Pauline church order. However unlikely this order may be now, it can be important today for an extraordinary situation in the missions and particularly in the field of ecumenism.

And so my theses run into questions which need to be discussed, and today more urgently than ever before. Could the present Church wish or be able to prevent that somewhere—a concentration camp, distant captivity without contact with the outside, an extraordinary missionary situation (e.g., in Communist China, or in the case of those Japanese Christians who lived for centuries without ordained pastors)—the same thing should happen that happened in Corinth and other Pauline communities, namely that guidance is simply provided by the free action of the Spirit of God through the charisms? When we assume the universal priesthood and the charismatic structure of the Church, should we still hold that the special apostolic succession via a series of impositions of hands is still the *only* and exclusive way into pastoral service, and should this be the only way in which we must think of apostolic succession? Even if this chain of impositions of hands is not taken so exclusively, would it still not remain an impressive sign of the apostolic succession in the pastoral line and therefore a sign of the unity, catholicity, and apostolicity of the Church? Would we then not have every reason to judge apostolic succession and the validity of the eucharistic celebration in those Churches that are not part of this "chain" of ordinations in a different and much more positive manner? Would this not help us to see also other questions, like that of the ordination of women or that of Anglican orders, in a new light? And if we do not, is it at all possible to do justice to the full spiritual life, the fruitful activity of pastors, men and women, of other churches? Is it then possible to mend the divisions of Christendom and to arrive at a mutual recognition? The enormous implications of these questions, both in theology and in the field of ecumenism, would seem obvious.

Translated by THEO WESTOW

NOTE

1. Cf. H. Küng, *The Church* (London, 1968), esp. Ch. D, IV, 2; E, II, 2.

3. Pro Intercommunion

To the various inquiries as to how common eucharistic celebrations by Catholics and Protestants are to be evaluated theologically, the following brief answer may be given.

1. Common celebrations of the eucharist must be viewed in a worldwide context. Such eucharistic celebrations in common have taken place in the most diverse places in Europe, America, and the Near East. These common eucharistic celebrations apparently have been an honest expression of a newly found unity between Christians of various confessional backgrounds, and also a new unity even in their Christian faith and understanding of the gospel message; a unity which does not preclude complete involvement in one's own Church; a unity which causes many of the differences in the outward structure of the Church to appear secondary. That many Catholics experience a stronger bond of unity in faith with open-minded Christians of other denominations than they feel with the close-minded Christians of their own confession is today a widespread phenomenon. This does not point to any internal breakup so long as the person remains committed to the unity of his own Church.

2. No weighty theological objections exist, in my estimation, against common celebration of the eucharist by Christians of different denominational background in two cases. (a) In the case of an *individual Christian,* who for good reasons (especially in a mixed marriage) or those extraordinary, if not absolutely rare, occasions when he participates in a eucharistic celebration of another denomination; in the case of a mixed marriage, for example, the reception of Holy Communion at the nuptial Mass would already be allowed the non-Catholic partner; so, according to principle, a corresponding procedure must be conceded ecumenically as a logical consequence. (b) In the case of communities where the common celebration in an extraordinary situation simply turns out to be, as it were, a charismatic event—without on that account already calling it institutionalization.

3. The refusal of such intercommunion by an appeal to canonical invalidity of the ecclesiastical office in respect to the ordination of the non-Catholic minister is untenable. This refusal seems to rest on the one hand on a narrow concept of apostolic succession, which

cannot mechanically and exclusively be dependent upon ordination (apostolic succession of the corporate Church, possible charismatic succession of individuals in the pastoral office); and, on the other hand, it depends on a clericalized misconception of ecclesiastical office and of its power of jurisdiction, which does not take seriously the common priesthood of all believers with regard to the celebration of the eucharist.

4. There will, nevertheless, be hesitation about institutionalized intercommunion of the denominations in the present situation. Such intercommunion suggests a unity between the separated churches which unfortunately at the present moment does not exist. We cannot disregard the consideration that ecclesiastical systems as such are still in many ways opposed to one another. We dare not make atonement too easy and too moderate for ourselves; we are already celebrating the communal meal together without having previously cleared away the serious obstacles that divide us, particularly the constitution of the Church. A premature institutionalized common eucharist gives an illusion of unity. Especially is it necessary that not only individuals, but the churches as well come to an understanding about the validity of ecclesiastical office in each other and that unity exist in their understanding of the eucharist: not a unity in theological explanation (for example, the teaching on transubstantiation) but rather a unity in belief by which all may say genuinely and candidly "Amen" to the words "The Body of Christ."

5. The shepherds (bishops, pastors) of the Church are urgently reminded of the ever-increasing instances of charismatic intercommunion: If you do not hasten with the ecumenical understanding more energetically than before, then you will more and more be charismatically pushed aside. The patience of many, not only of young people, not only of the intellectuals, is well known to be at an end. They are deeply disappointed by postconciliar ecumenical verbosity of many church officials and are no longer impressed by canonical and dogmatic arguments. An ecumenism of deeds must follow an ecumenism of words. Just to avoid confusion, just to arrive at a fundamental ecumenical approach and to allow intercommunion to be a real support for unity efforts, concrete actions must be immediately set in motion.

Concerning divine worship the following should be mentioned:

a. More frequent and not extraordinary common ecumenical services of the word as already conceded.

b. Wider freedom of choice in respect to participation in the eucharist in other Christian churches (especially for mixed marriages).

c. In the official mandate of the respective churches, examination of the terms for common, regular eucharistic celebrations of the denominations.

In preparation for the full eucharistic communion, the following are important:

a. Unreserved mutual recognition of baptism.

b. Regular exchange of preachers, catechists, and professors of theology for the purpose of mutual acquaintance with the common heritage and mutual aims.

c. The greatest possible common use of churches and common erection of churches and parish buildings.

d. Settlement of the mixed-marriage question through recognition of the validity of all mixed marriages and the leaving of the decision about baptism and rearing of the children to the conscience of the marriage partners (through an ecumenical marriage rite).

e. Advancement of common endeavors in Scripture study in the churches and in scientific knowledge (through common translation and commentary).

f. Intensified mutual efforts and integration of the denominational theological faculties (through merger of seminary libraries, common management of instruction).

g. Investigation of the possibilities of a common theological-ecumenical basic study (study of origins, fundamental theology).

h. Ecumenical co-operation in public life (common postures, initiatives and actions).

Translated by LEONARD W. BROUGHAN

4. Tribute to Karl Barth

Delivered at the funeral of Karl Barth in Basel

If I am permitted to speak as a Catholic theologian at the funeral of this great Protestant theologian, it is not only because I have been allowed for the last fifteen years to regard Karl Barth as my fatherly friend and constant spiritual companion, but also because Catholic theology itself should have a chance to speak at this grave. And I thank you for allowing this. Sorrowing with you today are countless Catholics, theologians and laymen, everywhere on earth where the word of Karl Barth has encountered them in so many languages.

There was a time which needed the *doctor utriusque iuris,* the doctor of both laws. Our time urgently needs the *doctor utriusque theologiae,* the doctor of both theologies, Protestant and Catholic. And if anyone in our century has offered an outstanding example of this, it was Karl Barth.

This may be surprising when we consider that hardly one important theologian of our century has attacked the Catholic Church and Catholic theology as positively, as angrily, and as defiantly as has Karl Barth—in his *Church Dogmatics* as surely as at the General Assembly of the World Council of Churches in Amsterdam. Yes, he challenged us Catholics to the right no less than neo-Protestant opponents to the left. And he opposed us not always in the tones of Mozart, of whom he asserted somewhat sadly in *Church Dogmatics,* notwithstanding his love, that he apparently was not an especially diligent Christian and moreover he was even Catholic. But his challenge was set forth for all its polemic with that quality which he so praised in Mozart—a great, passionate, free objectivity. And the subject for which he wished to obtain a hearing—a wide hearing—was the Christian message.

With the gospel as his starting point, he believed it necessary to speak so sharply, he believed it necessary to *protest* against us. And he seemed to many of us to be the Protestant theologian par excellence. But actually he protested not only when he was *against* something but when he was *for* something—something for which it was worth protesting even today and perhaps today even more so: for the wholly other living God whom a shallow Protestant and Catholic theology thinks it can completely capture within its human system; for the continuingly relevant word of God in Scripture, which even in the Church can be heard only with difficulty because of the merely pious and clever but all-too-human word, spoken and written; for the one Jesus Christ, whom people in the Church again and again are gladly willing to use for the support of another political or spiritual leader or even simply mankind itself; for the community of believing men, which again and again in the history of the Church is threatened either as an institution itself become powerful or as a fanaticism, arrogant and powerful.

With his positive protest, his great evangelical intentions, which must be maintained throughout, no matter what one's position regarding the Barthian system, Karl Barth has again made Protestant theology itself an earnest, evangelical discussion partner for us Catholics. And with this protest he has at the same time awakened many of us Catholics. His prophetic word, also in the *Dogmatics,* was heard in our church too, and he himself was surprised how well heard it was. Karl Barth, precisely as a fundamentally evangelical theologian in his influence even on the Catholic Church—very indirect and yet very effective (and to say this is no exaggeration)—has become one of the spiritual fathers of the Catholic renewal in connection with the Second Vatican Council, a renewal which in most recent years often permitted him to ask with mixed feelings of sadness and joy whether the Spirit of God was not as much alive in the Catholic Church as in his own.

But up to the end he did not think much of "Catholicization," that all too superficial self-adjustment, just as he also did not want his Catholic friends to "Protestantize." He warned against a repetition of Protestant mistakes in the postconciliar era. He expected others to have the same attitude he had, namely, not to get right off when one's own ship was in storm and peril but to get to work with trust in God's word, standing fast in one's own church but with a view toward the other.

He already had this open view. With it he had made it easier for us Catholic theologians to understand him and, through him, Protestant theology. And as he united a human, humorous gentleness with a relentless power of discernment, so he had also, with all his uncompromising Protestant emphasis, a theological breadth which allowed him to become a doctor of our theology also. It is this radical Protestant theologian who exhibits, despite differences, especially two characteristics which demonstrates Protestant-Catholic breadth above a narrow Protestantism.

For Karl Barth the *whole* Church was important, and this means first of all in its temporal dimension, even the Church of the past. He had long since opposed a historical view and a theological attitude which, in an unhistorical tie with the early Church, regards the interval between the early Church and the Reformation as an ecclesiastical vacuum. The foreword to volume I of *Church Dogmatics,* despite its clearcut rejection of the Catholic *analogia entis,* argues vigorously against those for whom church history begins with the year 1517 and who, as he says, based on the fairy tale of "sterile Scholasticism" and the catchwords of "the Greek thought of the Fathers of the Church" stop thinking precisely where the interesting problems begin. He wanted it to be permissible to refer to Anselm and Thomas "without any signs of disgust." Thus, Karl Barth, at once critical and understanding, stood in the Church of two thousand years, which in no century was absent from the world, joined with the great theologians whom he, constantly examining, still recognized as his fathers and brothers in the faith. He thereby acquired not only a Catholic breadth but also a Protestant substance. And precisely because he did not forsake continuity but took his stand with the Church and theology of the past, his criticism became so unignorable for us and so urgent.

For Karl Barth the *whole* Church was important, and that means then also in a spatial dimension: *the Church of the whole world.* Standing convinced in the Reformed tradition, and never rejecting Calvin as his particular church father, despite reservations, he had nothing in his theology and attitude of sectarian Protestantism as such. His theology was neither provincial nor, even worse, nationalistic. He did not think much of the introversion of boxed-in congregations, established churches, or even complacent confessional churches and alliances. Filled with the Pauline "care for all the churches," he realized in theory and practice a progressively universal outlook. And because he endeavored to think broadly, he was also widely listened to. He was universal in thought, and thus was able to bring about everywhere an evangelical emphasis. Thus he widely became—and this is perhaps the most beautiful thing we can say about him—a sign of our common faith. And precisely as such he was better able than anyone else to make the Reformation faith understandable to us, and this includes even the crucial and divisive

question of the Reformation 450 years ago, namely, the justification
of the sinner by faith alone, a question over which division is no
longer necessary today.

Many years ago we were discussing, as we did so often, the pope
and the Petrine office in the Church. And as he did not then agree
with me, I said smilingly, "Well, all right. I grant you good faith!"
Thereupon he became serious and said, "So you allow me good faith.
I have never conceded myself good faith. And when once the day
comes when I have to appear before my Lord, then I will not come
with my deeds, with the volumes of my *Dogmatics* in the basket
upon my back. All the angels there would have to laugh. But then I
shall also not say, 'I have always meant well; I had good faith.' No,
then I will only say one thing: 'Lord, be merciful to me a poor sinner!'"

That is the common belief of Christendom. And our comforting
hope is that Karl Barth will be given that for which prayed.

Translated by JAMES BIECHLER

LM: Do you still expect any official response? Is anything of this kind really to be expected?

KÜNG: No. From the very outset I assumed that there would be no official response. But I had really expected that my adversaries in the debate, who had been given such exhaustive answers, would once again have something to say. Since they have not yet done so, I assume that my comments have hit their target.

LM: From the Protestant standpoint the question of infallibility is not a central issue of theology. What place do you assign to it in the structure of theology as a whole?

KÜNG: We must distinguish here between the material and the formal aspects. In material terms the infallibility of the Church—or, more precisely, of the Church's magisterium—is a minor problem of ecclesiology. For Catholic theology, too, all that has to be said on God himself and Jesus Christ in relation to man takes precedence over this minor problem. And in this sense the question of infallibility is of slight importance. In fact it did not possess this importance from the beginning.

From the formal standpoint, however, infallibility is of the greatest importance, since it affects structurally all doctrinal statements, all dogmas and definitions. There is a difference between recognizing and professing the truth of a doctrinal statement in the light of an appeal to Scripture and the universal tradition, thus providing a material verification, and—on the other hand—an individual or a committee, a pope or a council being able to appeal to a presumed assistance of the Holy Spirit and therefore to make statements which on account of this assistance cannot a priori be false and thus are a priori absolutely true.

LM: Even the theological scholar will claim the assistance of the Holy Spirit. How much authority do you ascribe to scientific theology in comparison with the Church's magisterium?

KÜNG: We are here concerned with a different kind of function and therefore a different kind of authority. Even traditional Catholic theology distinguishes between the official authority of pope and bishops and the authority of the theologians as scholars. In traditional Catholic theology also we speak of a magisterium of the theologians, *a magisterium scientificum*. The recent declaration of the

5. Patiently Standing His Ground

On February 20, 1975, the Roman Congregation for the Doctrine of Faith published a final declaration in the proceedings which had been pending for years against Hans Küng. The latter was asked to stop spreading certain specific doctrinal opinions. The decision was regarded as unexpectedly mild. In his reactions therefore Küng avoided any appearance of polemical sharpness. Siegfried von Kortzfleisch led the present discussion on February 26 in Tübingen. LM.

LUTHERISCHE MONATSHEFTE: Five years ago, particularly with your book *Infallible?*, you started a debate out of which emerged what has come to be known as "the Küng case." The debate and the case have now more or less come to an end. What do you see as the fruits?

PROFESSOR KÜNG: They are of two kinds. The first relates to the proceedings. It has been possible to close this case in a way which surpasses the boldest hopes: that is, without a formal condemnation, without disciplinary measures—in particular, without the withdrawal of the Church's license to teach—and without the usual demand for retractation and submission. If that is not a reconciliation, it is at least a *modus vivendi*.

The second relates to the discussion. The discussion undoubtedly remains open. After the declaration *Mysterium Ecclesiae* of 1973, the Roman Congregation has once again made its position clear. It is entirely to be welcomed that a definite standpoint has been adopted on the Roman side. Nothing can be said against this. But it has also become clear that my questions have not been answered. For my own part, I have said everything that I had to say on the question of infallibility and on the magisterium. I published a kind of balance sheet in the miscellany *Fehlbar?—Eine Bilanz,*[1] in which other colleagues also expressed their reactions to various particular questions and in which I myself summed up at length the results of the debate. There has been no response so far to this volume and this "balance sheet," so that I can now quietly wait to see what further discussions will produce.

German bishops on the case—for the first time in an official announcement—made it clear that theology, too, has a critical function and is also expected to exercise it.

LM: Here obviously some progress has been made and the Roman Church can never go back on it.

KÜNG: This is true. There has been some progress here, although it goes against the grain a little with the officeholders, and in this connection the episcopal declaration cannot be merely negatively evaluated. I even wonder of whom in fact more is demanded: of me and my theology or of the Roman theology. If what is said in this document on "the necessity of a constant orientation of the life of the Church and theological study to the testimony of Scripture," on "historical-critical exegesis as a valuable and today indispensable aid," and on the manifold significance of the critical function of theology were also taken seriously in Roman theology, the latter would have to be fundamentally changed.

LM: If I may ask also about the positive aspect, what tasks of the Petrine office do you regard as the most important?

KÜNG: Quite fundamentally: If a Petrine ministry in the Church—and I prefer to speak of a Petrine ministry and not of the papacy—is to be credible, then it must keep to the guidelines of the biblical image of Peter and to the characteristics which are there ascribed in the diverse sources particularly to Peter. In this respect it is not a question of a succession understood juridically and historically, which it is very difficult to substantiate exegetically and historically, but of a factual-practical succession understood as a service to the community of the Church as a whole and to its unity. The important thing therefore would be for the Bishop of Rome to prove himself actually credible—as he sometimes did in the history of Christendom —as a rock of unity (cf. Matt. 16:18), as one who strengthens his brothers in faith (according to Luke 22:32), and as one who "feeds the sheep" (according to John 22:15–17) in a spirit of love and service.

LM: Could this perhaps be seen also beyond the frontiers of the Roman Church as it is at present? The American Lutherans and Catholics have indeed played with the idea that there could be a pope for all Christians, a pope "renewed in the light of the Gospel and

committed to Christian freedom." Do you think that the realization
of this lies within the realm of possibilities?

KÜNG: Why not? This American document is wholly on the lines of
what I wrote years ago in the books *Strukturen der Kirche* [*Structures of the Church*] (1962) and *Die Kirche* [*The Church*] (1967).
Here it is a question of something more than merely a primacy of
honor and also of more than a primacy of jurisdiction. What we are
talking about is a pastoral primacy, providing a pastoral service to
the whole Church. I think this is a very practical possibility. In the
person of John XXIII it proved to be at least partially realizable
even for Christians outside the Catholic Church. It would certainly
be useful for Christendom if there existed a center which could
mediate between the different regional and national churches, which
could provide inspiration—as John XXIII did in so many respects—
and also lead again to co-ordination and integration of the churches.
It would be essential for this service not to take the form of an exercise of power and not to be understood as such, but to be and to be
seen as a genuine act of service to the regional, national, and
denominational churches, so that the latter could be made to feel
that they were not being restricted or patronized but assisted and ad-
vanced.

LM: There is in fact a discrepancy between consensus and realization. Lutherans and Catholics have been able to note a very large degree of dogmatic agreement or closeness on hitherto apparently very
controversial points. What is known as the Malta Paper bears witness to this. But do you see any opportunities for these conclusions
to become really effective in the churches' practice?

KÜNG: I see not only opportunities but also clear results. Especially
if we look for them at the congregational level and not only at the
level of the large organization. There is no doubt at all today that the
relationship between the Catholic and Protestant congregations and especially between the Catholic parish priest and the Protestant pastor
on the spot is fundamentally different from what it was before the
Council. The development has even gone so far—particularly in the
Catholic Church—that we have reason to fear a serious estrangement
between the hierarchy on the one hand and the parishes and pastoral
clergy on the other. This will happen if there is no follow-up at the
level of the larger organization—that is, of the dioceses, the national

churches, and the Church as a whole—and if at this level certain truths which have long been taken for granted at the congregational level are not noted and certain demands for reform also taken for granted at the congregational level are not given the opportunity of being realized.

LM: What you have just explained also shows that the Roman Church is evidently not as homogeneous as perhaps it was at one time or in any case would still like to be. What is the significance of this diversity for the encounter with the diversity of the other denominations? Is it a weakness or perhaps even strength?

KÜNG: Certainly there are also weaknesses involved and I would prefer a greater uniformity in essentials. Perhaps the leaders should provide—as they usually did in the past—for reform measures to be carried out as far as possible in the Church as a whole and thus avoid the proliferation of uncontrolled experiments in individual congregations and regions. In principle, however, it is undoubtedly a question of strength, inasmuch as genuine Catholicity does not exclude diversity but in fact includes it. Today we have the opportunity of pluralism within the Church which is itself of the greatest importance for pluralism between the churches. For this ecumenical movement this means that pluralism between the churches should really become increasingly a pluralism within the Church. But this would presuppose our maintaining a basic unity in regard to the Christian message itself and to our faith and also in regard to certain main features of a church order and not moving from the one extreme of Roman authoritarianism and monolithic uniformism into a "Protestant" disarray in teaching and practice.

LM: But in this encounter of two plural factors is there not a danger that groups which happen to be sympathetic to one another will meet together, that people will seek out partners who are close to them anyway?

KÜNG: It is true that we have today a certain front which no longer runs *between* the denominations but cuts *right across* them, a new polarization between the more progressive and the more conservative forces in the different churches could scarcely be avoided. But we should nevertheless watch that we do not jump out of the frying pan into the fire and form still newer fronts in addition to those already existing. In that sense we should make absolutely certain—and this was also one of the concerns of my book *On Being a Christian*—of going ahead decisively with reforms, both in theory and in practice, but on the other hand of bringing out clearly what is essential to the Christian message and consequently to the Christian faith and of showing what is really important and what was to remain in the Church.

LM: At what distance do you set the goals for ecumenical efforts? Where do you place the long-term and where the medium-term goals?

KÜNG: Perhaps we cannot distinguish between long-term and medium-term goals as clearly as we can in financial policy, where we are concerned only with figures. For the long-term goal in any case is a Church in the sense described which contains plurality within itself but which, nevertheless, on the basis of the one message, the one baptism, and the one faith, is a community [*communio*] where no mutual exclusions [excommunications] are any longer necessary. Medium-term goals might involve a whole series of things which would result in a genuine, increasing integration of the different churches. I might specify: reform and mutual recognition of church ministries, common liturgy of the word and common weddings, open communion and increasingly also common eucharist or celebration of the Lord's Supper, common building and common use of churches and other buildings, common fulfillment of service to society, increasing integration of theological faculties and religious instruction, and finally also drawing up concrete plans for union by the church leaders at national and universal levels.

LM: Many of these goals however appear to be blocked at the moment. It is said that ecumenical relations are stagnating at many points. Is not even the term "stagnation" an understatement? In comparison with the first years after the Council, must we not speak even of clearly retrograde steps?

KÜNG: No. I would not say there has been any real regression. It is tantamount to a sign of hope that even the Roman Curia has not hitherto succeeded in reversing the developments. Even today, of course, there are people in Rome and elsewhere who would like to have the Latin Mass again. But in this respect as others it has not been possible anywhere to return to the status quo. What is certain, however, is that we are in a bottleneck. We do not really get far on the official level, and therefore we become increasingly involved in the polarizations already considered, between the ordinary people and the leadership of the churches.

At the same time, I am not thinking only of the Roman Curia. I am thinking also of the World Council of Churches, which—it seems to me—has concentrated far too one-sidedly on an ecumenism *ad extra* and reacted—rightly, to a large extent—to all possible problems in the world, but achieved far too little in regard to ecumenism *ad intra* and its original goal, the unity of the churches with one another. Here, as so often in politics, foreign policy has had to compensate for a not particularly successful home policy. I would like to add that there are some theologians who have not paid sufficient attention to the fact that we cannot set a credible example of ecumenism *ad extra* unless ecumenism *ad intra* is credibly put into effect. Far too many theologians thought that the traditional controversial questions were settled simply by leaving them aside. But, as the most recent discussions—for instance, on the recognition of ministries, intercommunion, papacy and infallibility, and so on—have clearly shown, the traditional controversial questions presuppose that we have found positive and constructive solutions to our own problems between the churches so that we can reach a consensus in faith and not merely cover up antagonisms which may break out afresh at any time.

LM: There are those who would like to pass over controversial problems; but there are certainly others, convinced of their own infallibility, who continually insist on the differences and on the fact that they themselves are in the right. Are there not similar claims to infallibility to be found also in Protestantism?

KÜNG: Certainly. I have always held that the problems of infallibility are common to all the churches. The problems that we have with the pope the Orthodox have analogously with their venerable Orthodox tradition; Protestantism has similar problems with the infallible Bible and now also with freedom of conscience and the claim of conscience on the part of the individual who seems occasionally to be more papal than the pope. In this respect I am quite happy that in our Church, despite the great tensions of the last ten years, we have largely been able to avoid any real sectarianism such as has created so much havoc in Protestantism and which has always come forward with a claim to infallibility.

LM: Is not the inclination of the churches to preserve themselves unavoidable? Is there not therefore also more or less built into every ecclesiastical institution a certain abnormal antiecumenical attitude?

KÜNG: Every institution tends to perpetuate itself and to expand according to certain laws—which have been very closely studied—and consequently it has considerable difficulty in accepting changes which seem to run contrary to this trend. Ecclesiastical institutions and their representatives are also inclined to maintain the status quo, and it is often possible to observe a singularly unholy "ecumenical" alliance between conservative Catholic and conservative Protestant church leaders. The result is that very often there is no settlement of the real differences or removal of defects on the part of the churches, but only resistance to uncongenial reforms, compensated by moral appeals to a very amoral society: appeals which demand little or nothing from the churches themselves.

LM: You want nothing else but to remain a Catholic. But could you not also imagine yourself a Protestant and thus a theologian in the other church? This, too, is a test of ecumenicity.

KÜNG: Do you think so? I have had many temptations in my life but not this one. In principle I do not attach much importance to individual conversions in either one direction or the other. I think it is important—and this I learned not least from Karl Barth—to stay in the boat during a storm and not to leave the steering to others. *Sauve qui peut*—even by getting onto another ship—is not the answer. For every Christian—Catholic or Protestant—the great task today is to deal with the situation in his own church and not to emigrate inwardly or outwardly. My own case in the Catholic Church has in fact shown precisely how rewarding it is, despite everything, to stand one's ground patiently and never to grow weary in the struggle for reforms. Fortunately it also becomes increasingly clear that, for the theologian committed to ecumenism, his own denomination loses its significance the more the common Christian cause gains in significance.

LM: The official Church has accused you of arguing from a standpoint outside the Catholic community of faith. You reject this change. But is it really possible to say so unequivocally to what extent someone is a Catholic?

KÜNG: Certainly we can no longer use the terms "Catholic" and "Protestant" to bring out the contrast between particular doctrines in the way that was possible in an age of denominationalism. But it seems to me important to be clear about the two *basic attitudes,* particularly if we want to achieve an integration. If I describe myself as a *Catholic,* I do so because I attach special importance to the Catholic—that is, to the entire, universal, all-encompassing, total—Church. Quite concretely: both to the continuity in time of faith and the community of faith enduring in all disruptions (tradition) and to the universality in space of faith and the community of faith embracing all groups. In other words, Catholicity in space and time.

If I were a *Protestant* theologian, I would respect the person who attaches special importance in all traditions, doctrines, and practices of the Church to constant, critical recourse to the gospel (Scripture) and to constant, practical reform in accordance with the norm of the gospel.

If we compare these two definitions, it becomes clear that Catholic and Protestant basic attitudes today are certainly not mutually exclusive. There are in fact an increasing number of Catholic theologians who would make this Protestant basic attitude their own and an increasing number of Protestants who would adopt this basic Catholic attitude. And in this sense we can see a growth in genuine ecumenicity particularly in theology and in practice. Quite concretely: an evangelical Catholicity finding its center in the light of the gospel or a Catholic "evangelicity" mindful of Catholic fullness. Expressed negatively, this would mean an ecumenical attitude against so-called "Protestant" radicalism and particularism, which must not be confused with Protestant radicalness and congregational attachment, and on the other hand an ecumenicity opposed to a "Catholic" traditionalism and syncretism, which must not be confused with Catholic tradition and fullness.

LM: You have looked for a way of remaining a Catholic without being Roman. Are there good reasons for such an attempt?

KÜNG: It seems to me that this way was found a long time ago and is in fact being followed by many Catholics. It is possible to have a completely positive approach to a Petrine ministry of the Bishop of

Rome and in that sense to an evangelically conceived "papacy." But this does not mean that it is necessary to be a Roman Catholic. As I explained some years ago in my book *The Church,* the expression "Roman Catholic" is a contradiction in terms and even in these terms is of very recent origin. What is required is for Rome to be Catholic, but not for the Catholic Church to be Roman.

Translated by EDWARD QUINN

NOTE

1. Zurich/Einsiedeln/Cologne, 1973.

IV. The Church and the Laity

1. Parties in the Church?

The question of parties in the Church is given different answers for different periods (New Testament, early Church, Middle Ages, Reformation, present), by different academic disciplines (politics and sociology, exegesis and history, systematic and pastoral theology), and by members of different confessions (Orthodox, Lutheran, Reformed, Anglican, Free Church, Catholic). Individual emphases vary widely.

A comprehensive and generally convincing answer seems difficult. On the other hand, the present distress of the churches in general and of the Catholic Church in particular calls for urgent efforts to examine and compare the conclusions of political scientists, exegetes, historians, theologians, and practitioners of all tendencies, to see if a concensus already exists or is at least in sight.[1]

A. Defining the Problem

1. *Parties in the Church are a real problem*

We fully expected some of the contributors to reject the problem of parties in the Church, either because they thought that it did not really exist in some churches now or in the early or medieval Church or because the question was simply unacceptable on theological grounds, parties in the Church being a priori a sin against the unity of the Church.

In fact, all the contributors, however they see the solution, agree that parties in the Church are a real problem. Indeed, the specialists in this sphere point out or take for granted that we are facing new polarizations in the Church. New tensions in the churches have replaced old tensions between the churches. These new tensions are problematical, but they also reveal new possibilities for ecumenism. Even in the Catholic Church, which in the period from the Counter-Reformation to Vatican II had a monolithic structure, strong polarizations and parties in one form or another are at least possible. The word "party" is used here in the broad sense of "tendency," "movement," "group," or "wing," whereas in section D below it will be used in the narrower sense of "political" party.

2. *The question is sharpened by the convergence of theological and sociological approaches*

From the point of view of theology, the Church has a special commitment to unity. This is stressed by all the contributors. Because of its basic Christian program, the Christian community cannot accept barriers of class, race, culture, or education, but attempts instead to include tensions and contradictions that are sociopolitical ("master-slave"), cultural ("Greek-barbarian"), and sexual ("man-woman"). This all-embracing unity is already basically achieved and manifested in eucharistic communion. From the point of view of sociology, however, the Church is also a human organization and not exempt from the sociological laws which bind all human organizations and for this reason the possibility of parties in the Church cannot be excluded in advance.

In its sharpest form, the question runs as follows: Can a community whose aim is to embrace and transcend parties in society, including modern political parties, admit parties within itself, ecclesial parties?

3. *Theological, liturgical, and disciplinary pluralism in the Church is legitimate*

There is also false unity. Pluralism can be a source of freedom and creativity in the Church. The diamond of Christian truth has many facets; difference is not bad, only difference hardened into exclusiveness. Since the Second Vatican Council, the need and value of a complex pluralism is no longer disputed even within the Catholic Church but vigorously affirmed: diversity in teaching, liturgy, and organization, arising out of diversity in language, culture and ways of thought, philosophical and cultural categories, different religious experiences, and different selections from the New Testament. On all sides, and most strongly from the Eastern and Anglican churches, there is a desire not for a uniform but for a pluriform Church.

In this quarter, then, there are no obstacles to allowing the application to the Church of terms such as "movement," "GROUP," "tendency," and "wing." Parties (in the broad sense) in the Church are acceptable without qualification (and even to some extent desirable) when this term covers groups which differ from each other and are not in conflict but in communion with each other. These movements may be missionary, biblical, liturgical, or catechetical. They may be movements for peace and justice, national, ethnic, racial, and social groupings, different religious orders or communities, associations, and organizations of all sorts. There will be room in the Church of the future for "parties" which bring a variety of groups into fruitful interaction and yet maintain community among them.

4. *Pluralism in the Church has limits*

Pluralism can be a danger to the unity and continued existence of the Church. Today Protestants, too, stress more than they did in the past the need for the unity of the Church in the face of so many attempts to further particular interests in the Church. Eastern Christians encourage the formation of groupings in the Church provided that they do not separate from the mother church and set themselves up as churches. Even the Anglican Church, which openly accepts parties, has some limits—a church in which all possible views could be taught would not be the Church of Christ. Indifferent pluralism would destroy the character of the Church as the community of believers. Pluralism may be accepted, but promiscuity is rejected. A community that wants to survive needs at least a minimum consensus. Just as democracy cannot be abolished in the name of democracy, neither can the plural Church in the name of ecclesial pluralism.

However much the Church may tolerate various movements, groups, tendencies, and wings, there is general agreement that it cannot tolerate sects which cut themselves off from it. Definitely unacceptable (and indeed harmful, even if not always easy to eliminate) are parties in the Church which seal themselves off and separate themselves from the community and its faith and life. These parties include all sects, in other words, whether they are based on theology, race, culture. In the Church of the future there can therefore be no parties which bring alienation and dissension into the church community.

5. *The final criterion of unity and plurality in the Church is Jesus Christ himself*

Because of this ambiguity, because many parties are neither definitely acceptable nor definitely unacceptable but a question, because parties can exist in the Church which remain in community with each other but are also in conflict, further clarification is necessary. Notwithstanding any political commitment on the part of the Church or its members, a political ideology, whether Marxist or capitalist, Communist or Fascist, can never be the decisive criterion for the church community. The decisive criterion for the church community, for the necessary unity and possible plurality, can for the Church of Jesus Christ be only Jesus Christ himself, as the New Testament testifies. Today this point is stressed equally by Catholics, and Protestants, even if it is expressed in different words. Examples of this are "the person and mission of Jesus," "the gospel of Jesus Christ," "the Lord of the Church," which is the "Body of Christ." If, then, the norm for the Church as the community of those who believe in Christ is Christ himself, clearly all dogmas, rites, and organized forms, and all theologies and structures, must be open to reform and correction. *Ecclesia semper reformanda* of course presupposes *Ecclesia semper eadem*, reform without a change of identity.

B. Principles of a Solution

1. *There are groups in the New Testament which can be called parties*

The Judaism of Jesus' time was already familiar with religious parties. Best known are the *haireseis* or "parties" of the Sadducees, Pharisees, and Nazarites, groups which took an individual position on certain important religious questions, without renouncing their allegiance to Judaism like the heretical (in the negative sense) "sect" of the Samaritans.

Therefore the Church, too, which is based on Jesus Christ, has from the beginning existed in various groups, which in contemporary terminology may certainly be called "parties" (*haireseis*) because they were based on different "teachings." The primitive Jerusalem community has "Hebrews" and "Hellenists," and later the exclusively Jewish Christian group in Jerusalem took a harder line and insisted on observance of the Jewish law by all. The Antioch group regarded the Jewish law as abolished in Christ and practiced a mission to the Gentiles which ignored the law. There were also further distinctions between the stricter (James) and more liberal (Peter) Jewish Christians, between communities willing to compromise (James's Antioch formula) and the uncompromising apostle Paul, in whose communities old and perhaps also new parties emerged (though in Corinth they may have been not so much theological parties as factions which grew up around particular individuals on personal grounds).

2. *These parties are not so much the result of human sin as of the preaching of the gospel in a diverse sociocultural context*
It was inevitable that the preaching of the gospel to all nations and all men should have different results—particularly as regards the form of the preaching and observance of the Jewish law—in areas of traditional Jewish thought and in the wide area of Hellenistic Judaism in the diaspora. These groupings led to party spirit, opposition, and tension in theory and practice which was probably just as strong as what we know today.

3. *Nevertheless the individual communities remained linked in a unity which did not allow a division in the Church*
The foundation of this unity was confession of one God and one Lord, Jesus Christ, and thus one faith, one baptism, and one Lord's Supper. Even the uncompromising Paul warned against divisions (*schismata*), appealed for a common mind, and was in word and deed in the forefront of the fight for the unity of his communities among themselves and with Jerusalem. "Is Christ divided?" was his battle cry. Nevertheless, right from the beginning this unity was not a matter of uniformity but consisted in communication between Christian groups, the transmission of different theological traditions, the adaptation of attitudes and argument about Jesus Christ, the standard of faith, who was not the permanent possession of any one group but was constantly having to be rediscovered in new situations.

4. *As well as the different parties within the church community there were groups which not only interpreted the gospel differently but preached a different gospel*
To be distinguished from the parties within the Church are the true sects, *haireseis* in the firmly negative sense, which shut them-

selves up in their own tradition and language and do not communicate with the church community. Not only Paul but other writers of the New Testament and several apostolic Fathers attack such separatist groups.

5. *According to the New Testament, the existence of parties in the Church is permitted not for the sake of divisions but for the increase of commitment to the Lord and his Church*

The formation of groups is permitted and desired as an aid to unity and communication, for the building up of the community and for mission, and especially for the service of men. The existence of parties of this type with a special commitment gives groups a more definite character but does not destroy unity. It promotes toleration within the Church but does not make it more difficult to excommunicate those who reject communication in the Church.

C. The Lessons of History

1. *Throughout the whole history of the Church there have been dieval Church true parties with a theological basis*

These groups have tended towards theology or social affairs, church politics or spirituality. There have also been, from the beginning, groups which, because they have emphasized a particular interest, have separated themselves from or have been forced out of the Church.

2. *From the fourth century in particular there were in the early medieval Church true parties with a theological basis*

These were not, as in the past, groups with a particular theology sharply distinguished from the Church as a whole. Now the whole episcopate was divided into changing groups which defended their positions with propaganda literature, by furthering special interests, or by mutual accusation and changing coalitions. The struggle centered on the filling of episcopal appointments. Nevertheless a permanent secession by large groups was avoided in the fourth century.

3 *A common concern can be seen behind the various contradictory theological formulations*

Of great importance for the preservation of church unity amid all the party struggles was the conciliatory policy of various bishops, and especially Athanasius, who avoided blind partiality and never lost sight of the issue which lay behind and beyond disputed formulas. In this way the various parties were able to recognize the different terminology of other parties as possible and legitimate, and no more was asked than acceptance of the Nicene creed and condemnation of the old heresies. And these parties had positive as well as negative results—they contributed to a more comprehensive understanding of the truth. Not only heretical isolationism but also ultraorthodox zeal has often held up the discovery of truth and inflicted fruitless party battles on the Church.

4. *In the complexity of the historical situation, it is difficult to discern the boundary between the true faith and heresy, between a party within the Church and a sect.*

Both in the teaching and practice of the Church actual historical situations include an infinity of tendencies and divergences, affinities and tensions, connections and distinctions. Concealed rigorism and reconciled heresy, influence, aggression, and delicate balancing factors make a judgment difficult. The ambiguity of the word *hairesis* reflects the ambiguity of situations.

5. *Especially since the High Middle Ages, it has been impossible to ignore the socioeconomic influences on many movements, parties, and even divisions in the Church*

There can be no neat separation between Church and society, theology and politics. Neither churches nor sects, faith or heresy, can be analyzed without taking into account their social roots. There is what might be called a sociological justification for heresy. Economic prosperity, the development of free towns and independent universities, the new ideas of class, and increased mobility have influenced ecclesiastical and theological parties just as conversely the religious appeal to the people, the gospel for the poor, the idea of brotherhood, the new ethos of work, and apocalyptic expectations have influenced social developments and divisions. Evangelical and political movements have often run side by side and they have always depended and reacted on each other, often with mutual confusion.

6. *An authoritarian Church provokes opposition from within*

From the High Middle Ages onwards, a very diverse opposition

grew up on the part of individuals and groups. It had a socioeconomic as well as a spiritual and theological character, and directed itself against a hierarchy which had identified itself with the feudal system and had thereby become rich and authoritarian. How dangerous
this often ambivalent appeal to the gospel and new social factors was
to become, did not become clear until the Late Middle Ages and the
Reformation.

7. *The split between East and West was essentially the result of a rejection of the pluralism traditionally practiced in the united Church*

Unity in the Western Church came increasingly to be understood
as uniformity. This led not only to an internal hardening but also to
external isolationism, in the form of a slow drift away from the Eastern churches, which finally became a breach which has still not been
mended. The existence of Eastern churches which differ in form
amongst themselves and have an equal claim with Rome to direct
apostolic origin is a challenge to the Western Church, and in particular to the papacy, to rethink plurality in the teaching, liturgy, and
constitution of the Church and to make room for it in genuinely
collegial structures.

8. *Luther saw himself as a reformer within the Church, but was
forced to accept a division in the Church for the sake of the gospel*

There can be historical moments in which criticism must be expressed and protest registered in the sharpest possible way. Luther
did not want a breach in the community of the Church, but he did
want obedience to the gospel. Since this controversy was clearly
about essential elements of the Christian message, the result was not
the secession of a fringe group but a split, this time down the middle
of the Western Church. Parties within the Church became two
different expressions of the Christian Church. To this extent we can
talk of a "hierarchy of parties," parties based on superficial matters
and those based on essentials.

9. *The existence of parties within a single church (as notably in the
Anglican) is assessed differently even within this church.*

The Anglican Church gradually came to be divided into three parties—high, low, and broad church. What was still regarded in the
seventeenth century as a necessary evil or even sin has since the
nineteenth century been regarded as an advantage and an advance,

though there have always been protests from Anglo-Catholics. In our own century the Anglican Church has often been put forward as a model of what ecumenical efforts should aim at, as a "bridge church" between different tendencies. However, this argument has not been generally accepted either inside or outside the Anglican Church.

D. A Systematic Solution Today

1. *Current terminology is dominated by the concept of political party (i.e., "party" in the narrower sense)*

"Party" in the narrower sense does not today mean a separatist sect, but neither does it mean merely a tendency, movement, or group ("party" in the broad sense). A party in the narrower sense has the following characteristics. It seeks to take over and exercise political power, to achieve specific aims in social welfare and prevent others from being achieved. It puts forward programs and candidates for elections and has a permanent organization.

2. *Whether such parties should be formed in the Church is not a dogmatic but primarily a political question*

The history of political parties and their origin is closely connected with the development of the franchise and its extension to broader sections of the population. Where elections are allowed, the formation of parties is a normal development, and they have always been concerned with putting up candidates for parliamentary assemblies and winning elections. As a rule, every parliament has formal groupings (for the orderly conduct of debates and divisions) and parties (at least for electoral purposes). The setting up of collegial or synodal bodies in the Catholic Church in parishes and dioceses, at national and (on a limited scale) universal level, with at least some elected members therefore makes it possible to form organized groups within these bodies and parties for elections to them.

Acceptance or rejection of parties in the narrower sense does, of course, have theological implications. On the one hand, for example, it makes the priesthood of all believers a reality and, on the other, it preserves church unity. But the question as to whether these theological goals should be attained by means of ecclesiastical parties or without them is a practical question. In answering it, however, the political implications of such parties must be borne in mind. There is, for example, a need for an efficient party organization and at least a rudimentary bureaucracy and party propaganda. Members have to be recruited and party activities have to be financed. Parties may acquire a momentum of their own, and this can only to a limited degree be regulated by the parent organization (in this case the Church).

3. *There are arguments for parties in the Church*
Organized parties in the Church would make it possible: (a) for the laity to share responsibility without the present feeling of impotence and frustration; (b) to settle, in an orderly and public way, the conflicts which cannot be avoided in any healthy society, on the basis of shared convictions and ideals; (c) to educate church members through the information and discussion which goes with the existence of parties. This is of particular importance in a time of rapid social change in the Church and pressure for it to adapt to new situations.

4. *There are arguments against parties in the Church*
Organized parties in the Church would make it possible: (a) for particular religious differences to become institutions, be made absolute and be perpetuated; (b) permanent hostility to arise between persons and groups, a weakening and perhaps leading to the collapse of communications between the parties and giving rise to new divisions in the Church; (c) for Church parties to be confused with political parties and systems, which vary so widely in different countries.

5. *In particular situations the formation of parties or at least of groups may be unavoidable*
Since the situations in different countries, with different political systems and levels of development, are extremely varied, it is hardly possible to suggest a general solution. In the past, an authoritarian and undemocratic church system has often given rise to a sharp polarization, the formation of parties, and even divisions, and this may happen again today. Above all, the connection of ecclesiastical authority with established political power and its refusal to accept political or social commitment may lead to the formation of groups engaged in contestation. Sometimes, as the result of particular traditions and dispositions of power, a particular group uses spiritual (and also legal and financial) power as a subtle or sometimes even

brutal means to maintain a status quo advantageous to itself and to prevent serious reforms in Church and society. This one-party church is not the best advertisement for unity and order in the Church.

In this way the formation of a group, or eventually an organized party, within the Church may be unavoidable. For example, when bishops in a synod form a bloc, a counterbloc is almost always formed, and this will in time have effects on the situation in the Church outside the synod. When a central Roman administration attempts to restore its feudal and absolutist power over the Church's teaching and practice in a democratic age, sharp polarizations, internal disaffection of large sections of the population from Rome, and open conflicts are to be expected.

6. *If possible, organized groups and parties in the Church should be avoided*

From a political point of view, it is not certain whether the advantages to Church and mankind of group and party formation outweigh the disadvantages. Certainly the tactics, propaganda, and campaigning methods used by political parties can hardly be a model for the Church.

From the theological point of view, it is appropriate that a community whose aim is to embrace and transcend social antagonisms and political parties should not add its own (interchurch or intrachurch) antagonisms to those of society. In some circumstances these take the form of hot or cold wars of religion. It is better for a community of faith, love, and prayer to express its spiritual unity as free agreement and mutual openness.

In view of the well-known inadequacies of the political-party system, it may be possible to find other, no less effective, models of decision-making for the Church which are more appropriate to it. Questions of faith can hardly be solved by purely majority decisions. In any case, decisions in church synods have usually been sought through consensus—not a mathematical but a moral unanimity—which means leaving disputed questions open. Even during Vatican II, though votes were necessary, efforts were made to reach this sort of unanimity, and in spite of the variety of tendencies no parties or fixed groups in the end emerged. As a means of avoiding the undesirable developments of the party system, there might be practical and legal advantages in having direct voting for specific candidates instead of a proportional system with party lists. In this system the fundamental choice could be limited to the local community or small region, and representatives to the synods chosen from the local and regional assemblies.

7. *Pluralism between churches could become pluralism within the Church*

Even if the formation of groups and parties in the churches is often unavoidable in practice, the terrible experiences of the past make it vital to avoid fundamental divisions in the Church—even for the sake of the gospel. The unfortunate handling by both sides of the Reformation should not be taken by either side as a model for future cases.

The old days must not return. Today all the various churches seek together and concentrate on the essence of the gospel as a means to give scope to the diversity of understanding of the one gospel. Ecumenism is indivisible. It applies *ad intra* and *ad extra,* and must start in its own church if it wants to enlighten the *oikoumenē.* We should work towards a situation in which distinctions between Catholics, Orthodox, Anglicans, and Protestants of various tendencies become parties or tendencies within the Church, groups which are different but no longer far apart, but rather in full community with each other. At this stage a common celebration of the Lord's Supper by the different churches should be considered. At the same time, and with an eye to the more distant future and the other great world religions, the possibility should also be considered of recognizing Hindu Christians and Buddhist Christians with their rich traditions (critically examined) within one Christian Church.

What has to be done to overcome polarizations in the churches and between the churches? We must expose ourselves fully to Christ and his gospel and together look at God and our fellow men and accept all the consequences of this attitude. We must be open to the Spirit and in sympathy with each other whenever we differ. We must learn to speak more freely to each other and to listen to each other in vital questions of faith. We must keep a sense of proportion, which was so characteristic of the first Christian witnesses, have a deeper understanding of the different spiritual gifts with their importance for the life of the Church as against one-sided and exclusive theologies, and take seriously the plurality of cultures and the resulting pluriformity in the expression of the Christian faith. We must try

Parties in the Church? 131

to understand more deeply the conciliar process through which the Church lived in the past and in which it will find new life. We must practice, together with the priestly ministry of liberating reconciliation, the prophetic ministry of liberating reconciliation, the prophetic ministry of liberating conflict and learn to conquer all conflicts which divide the Church and the nations in the last resort through the cross of Christ.

Translated by FRANCIS MCDONAGH

NOTE

1. My colleagues in the Institute for Ecumenical Research at the University of Tübingen Dr. Hermann Häring and my doctoral student Karl-Josef Kuschel have read and discussed all the articles in this issue of *Concilium* with me. The subject was also discussed earlier in our doctoral students' colloquium, in which Professor Dr. Theodor Eschenburg, among others, took part.

2. Participation of the Laity in Church Leadership and in Church Elections

A. A Blind Spot in the Decree on the Laity

The theme to be treated here is, surprisingly, not to be found in the Vatican II Decree on the Apostolate of the Laity. That fact makes the matter difficult. Participation, co-operation, collaboration of the laity in the decisions of the Church? People like to talk of the participation of the laity in the *life* (not the decisions) of the Church. They also like to speak of the participation of the laity in the decisions of the *world* (but not of the Church). They do not at all like to speak, at least in official binding documents, of the participation of the laity in the *decisions* of the *Church*. Nevertheless it is precisely here that the question of the status of the laity in the Church arises in the most practical way. For, as long as I can contribute advice and work but am excluded from decision-making, I remain, no matter how many fine things are said about my status, a second-class member of this community: I am more an object which is utilized than a subject who is actively responsible. The person who can advise and collaborate but not participate in decision-making in a manner befitting his status, *is* not really the Church but only *belongs to* the Church. Yet this idea contradicts the very understanding of "laity" as we have once again seen it in the past decades, not least in Vatican II itself. It is not necessary here to go into the problematic of the somewhat unfortunate term "laity"; we not infrequently compensate for it by the use of such terms as "church" or "congregation," in contrast to the "shepherds" (presiding officers) or the "pastoral offices" (the supervisory offices).

Unfortunately the Decree on the Apostolate of the Laity of Vatican II, which carries on in a very long-winded and paternal fashion on various subjects which are quite obvious, remains on this point, which is so decisive in practical life, far behind what Yves Congar had already pioneered with concrete possibilities in the difficult preconciliar days by his courageous and epoch-making *Jalons pour une théologie du laïcat*.[1] Did this happen solely because this decree on the Apostolate of the Laity came about without the active participation of the laity itself in the decision-making and thus is essentially a product of clerics? Well, even Yves Congar is not a layman but a cleric. That the decree has here a blind spot should not so much be ascribed to the clergy as clergy as to the clericalism of the clergy, a trait which can also be found among the laity.

The basis for joint decision in the Church was itself laid out thoroughly in the decree, inasmuch as in the first section of the first preparatory chapter it was said that the laity "share in the priestly, prophetic, and royal office of Christ" and that from thence they "have their own role to play in the mission of the whole People of God in the Church and in the world" (Art. 2). And at the same time the decree alludes to the pertinent section of the Constitution on the Church, which will be reproduced here in full, because it explains in a concise, beautiful and constructive way the basis on which our later reflections are grounded:

> Therefore, the chosen People of God is one: "one Lord, one faith, one baptism" (Eph. 4:5). As members they share a common dignity from their rebirth in Christ. They have the same filial grace and the same vocation to perfection. They possess in common one salvation, one hope, and one undivided charity. Hence, there is in Christ and in the Church no inequality on the basis of race or nationality, social condition or sex, because "there is neither Jew nor Greek; there is neither slave nor freeman; there is neither male nor female. For you are all 'one' in Christ Jesus" (Gal. 3:28; cf. Col 3:11).
>
> If therefore, everyone in the Church does not proceed by the same path, nevertheless all are called to sanctity and have received an equal privilege of faith through the justice of God (cf. 2 Pet. 1:1). And if by the will of Christ some are made teachers, dispensers of mysteries, and shepherds on behalf of others, yet all share a true equality with regard to the dignity and to the activity common to all the faithful for the building up of the Body of Christ.
>
> For the distinction which the Lord made between sacred ministers and the rest of the People of God entails a unifying purpose, since pastors and the other faithful are bound to each other by a mutual need. Pastors of the Church, following the example of the Lord, should minister to one another and to the other faithful. The faithful in their turn should enthusiastically lend their cooperative assistance to their pastors and teachers. Thus in their diversity all

bear witness to the admirable unity of the Body of Christ. This very diversity of graces, ministeries, and works gathers the children of God into one, because "all these things are the work of one and the same Spirit" (1 Cor. 12:11) [Art. 32].[2]

Now if this is all true—and it is true—then the question arises spontaneously: If the community of all those in the Church goes so deep in spite of all differences of gifts and services that it is not possible to go deeper, then why, considering the communality of the one Lord, of the one Spirit and the one Body, of one faith and one baptism, of one grace and vocation, of one hope and love, and finally of one responsibility and task—why then, despite all the diversity of functions, is there not also in the Church a communality of *decision?* On this one point the Constitution on the Church as well as the Decree on the Apostolate of the Laity remains timid. The medieval and post-Tridentine past still casts its long, heavy shadows upon them. It was in fact seen as great progress that the laity, who since Trent, or actually only since Vatican I, had been excluded from the Councils, were again admitted at least in trifling numbers as auditors (the listening Church!). Vatican I was a council of the pope, Vatican II a council of the bishops (and the theologians); as such they were great councils. But only Vatican III, it remains to hope, will be a council of priests and laity. The bishops fought courageously for collegiality: but only on the level of the universal Church over against papal absolutism (papalism) and not on the level of the diocese over against its own similarly entrenched episcopal absolutism (episcopalism). Here is the task of the future, which some bishops already perceive. The Constitution of the Church (especially Arts. 33–38)—and very much less clearly the Decree on the Laity (especially Arts. 10, 20, 23–26), which was also decided upon by the hierarchy—speak of course at great length and often still in an extremely paternalistic manner (with "fatherly love" the laity are addressed as the extensions and representatives of the clergy) of the much-desired activity and collaboration of the laity, of involvement and encouragement, recognition and the fostering of the laity, of the usefulness of their advice and their experience. How laboriously and repeatedly the "concessions" to the laity had to be wrung almost word by word from the traditionalistic curial group for the decree on the laity as well as for the chapter on the laity of the Constitution on the Church is impressively shown by the excellent commentary by Ferdinand Klostermann.[3]

There is also repeatedly in the documents talk of possible agencies or lay councils (e.g., Constitution on the Church, Art. 37; Decree on the Apostolate of the Laity, Art. 26), which, however, according to the assertions of the documents, seem to have no more than an advisory function. The following passage from the Constitution on the Church is typical of the great openness and at the same time the time-bound narrowness of Vatican II:

> Let sacred pastors recognize and promote the dignity as well as the responsibility of the layman in the Church. Let them willingly make use of his prudent advice. Let them confidently assign duties to him in the service of the Church, allowing him freedom and room for action. Further, let them encourage the layman so that he may undertake tasks on his own initiative. Attentively in Christ, let them consider with fatherly love the projects, suggestions, and desires proposed by the laity. Furthermore, let pastors respectfully acknowledge that just freedom which belongs to everyone in this earthly city.
>
> A great many benefits are to be hoped for from this familiar dialogue between the laity and their pastors: in the laity, a strengthened sense of personal responsibility, a renewed enthusiasm, a more ready application of their talents to the projects of their pastors. The latter, for their part, aided by the experience of the laity, can more clearly and more suitably come to the decisions regarding spiritual and temporal matters. In this way, the whole Church, strengthened by each one of its members, can more effectively fulfill its mission for the life of the world [Art. 37].

This passage says much which was never found before in this form in official documents, and to that extent there has been a breakthrough to a new communality and community in the Church. But the passage is also steadfastly silent on the question which must not be avoided or overlooked: If the laity are to be included as advisors and collaborators, then why not also as decision-makers?

B. Fundamental Principles

But are there perhaps serious theological objections, and not merely a centuries-long tradition of clericalism in the Catholic Church, which do indeed favor the participation of the laity in advis-

ing and working but not in decision-making in the Church? Is this
not perhaps a misunderstanding of the real essence of the Church,
which is grounded not on a free accord of a believing individual but
on the call by God in Christ? Has not an essential differentness—a
differentness which does not admit a translation of the modern democratic model to the Church—been overlooked? Has not the hierarchical character of the Church, which is built upon the apostles and
the apostolic succession of the office-bearers and thus excludes any
democratization, been forgotten? These and similar serious considerations should be answered, and of course not simply from the
conciliar decrees, which in their treatment of this question have
remained superficial, but from the original Christian message, as it
expressed itself and operated in the Church or the churches of the
original New Testament age. What was originally correct cannot later
on be rejected as false in principle by those who call themselves followers.

   1. If we may, to begin with, argue from a more sociological point
of view: Some of those who today reject joint decision-making with
the laity in the Church earlier rejected on the same basis any serious
participation of the laity through collaboration and advising in the
Church. And some of those who protest today against a democratization of the Church and against any translation of secular sociological
models to the Church not too long ago accepted without reflection the
secular sociological model of the monarchy for the Church, and even
in practice did nothing against the monarchization of the Church.
They found no contradiction to the brotherhood of the New Testament[4] in conducting themselves in practice as monarchs, for the most
part bound in no way by a constitution but for all practical purposes
absolute monarchs: petty and sometimes even very great and mighty
kings and lords in their parishes ("Monsignor," i.e., "My Lord"), dioceses ("Your Graces," "Excellencies," and "Eminences"), and in
the universal Church ("Summus Pontifex" and "King of Kings and
Lord of Lords"). This is not to say anything against the past, but it
is past! In some countries Catholics even in this century opposed in
every way possible the introduction of democratic forms into secular
society in the name of this "divinely established" monarchical hierarchy, and Leo XIII was actually disgracefully insulted by ultra-
Catholics when he finally abandoned the scruples of the hierarchical
Church towards the democratic form of government. In a nutshell:
The man who has nothing against the monarchization of the Church

can really not have anything of a decisive theological nature against the democratization of the Church. Basically it is better even in the Church to speak of a democracy (the entire holy People of God) than of the "hierocracy" (a holy caste). For while in the New Testament all worldly honorary titles are strictly shunned in connection with bearers of office, they are in fact given to the entire believing people, which is designated "a chosen race, a royal priesthood, a consecrated nation" (1 Pet. 2:9), and made "a line of kings and priests, to serve our God and to rule the world" (Rev. 5:10).

But that already demonstrates that in decisive matters we are careful to argue not in sociological but in theological categories. Only in this way can we show that joint decision-making and regulation on the part of the laity is not only a timely concession to modern democratic developments but is a move thoroughly rooted in the Church's own origins. This is not to deny that the modern democratic development has not ultimately helped the Church break out of her traditionalistic clerical encrustations and reflect on her original structure. Here a comparison with the democratic state can be helpful: As the citizens not only belong to the state but in a full sense *are* the state, so all Church members in a full sense are the Church; they are all not mere inhabitants but full citizens of the Church. Instead of this, the traditional concept of the Church with its two-class theory, especially as it has operated since the Constantinian era in the entire ecclesiastical area, and after the Gregorian reform in its ultraclerical form, has relied mostly on other models. Among these models were the monarchist state (more frequently of an imperial-absolute style): ruler and ruled, commander and obedient; or the family: adults and minors, fathers and children; or the school: teachers and pupils (listeners); or property: owners (masters) and nonowners (servants).[5]

But can it be that the essence of the Church seen from a theological perspective necessarily demands two classes or ranks, especially as the Code of Canon Law in Canon 107 orders that "by virtue of divine institution" the clerics are to be differentiated from the laity in the Church?[6] A further clarification is necessary.

2. Out of a correct—that is to say, biblical and historical—perspective of "apostolic succession" there arises the question of the joint role of the laity in the decision-making in the Church.[7] Here this can be indicated only briefly.[8] The special and unquestionable apostolic succession of the multiple pastoral service (the bishops

with the pope, but in their way also the pastors with their co-
workers) must not be isolated but must be seen in its functionality:

a. The Church *as a whole* (Credo Ecclesiasm apostolicam!), and
thus each individual church member, also stands in succession to the
apostles. In what sense? The Church, as well as all individuals,
remains bound to the basic witness and service of the original
witnesses without which there would be no Church. The Church is
founded on the apostles (and the prophets). All the faithful thus are
supposed to succeed the apostles in apostolic faith and confessing,
life and service. This service takes the most diverse forms of proclamation, baptism, the community of prayer and the Supper, the
building up of the congregation, and service to the world.

b. The special apostolic succession of the diverse *pastoral service,*
important as it is, is not thereby an end in itself. The pastoral service
continues the special task of the apostles, in which they differentiate
from other important and likewise permanent services in the Church,
such as that of the prophets or the teachers: namely, to establish and
guide the churches. From this service of guiding the Church, these
office-bearers (bishops, pastors, further co-workers) also have a special authority; only in service can their authority have any foundation at all. The shepherds in the Church are thus in no way a management class with a unilateral imperial power, toward which the
single possible attitude is unilateral obedience. They are no *domin-
ium* but a *ministerium*. They form no power structure but a special
service structure. "You know that among the pagans their so-called
rulers lord it over them, and their great men make their authority
felt. This is not to happen among you. No; anyone who wants to become great among you must be your servant, and anyone who wants
to be first among you must be slave to all. For the Son of Man himself did not come to be served but to serve, and to give his life as a
ransom for many" (Mark 10:42–45).

So the purpose of shepherds in the Church is special service to the
apostolic Church which is made up of all the believers. For this
reason the term "hierarchy" or "holy rule" (customary only since
the time of Dionysius the Pseudo-Areopagite, five hundred years
after Christ) is misleading. To be relevant biblically, it is better to
speak of "diakonia" or "church service."

For the nurturing and constant growth of the People of God,
Christ the Lord instituted in His Church a variety of ministries,
which work for the good of the whole body. For those ministers

who are endowed with sacred power are servants of their brethren, so that all who are of the People of God, and therefore enjoy a true Christian dignity, can work toward a common goal freely and in an orderly way, and arrive at salvation. [Constitution on the Church, Art. 18.]

Thus if from a biblical perspective the shepherds are not the masters but the servants of the Church or the congregation (= the "laity"), why then should it in practice be possible to exclude the Church or the congregation (= the "laity") from joint decision-making? This can happen only if the shepherds are seen not as the servants of the Church, but as its exclusive owners or fathers or teachers.

But the shepherds are *not* the *owners* of the Church, toward whom laity are only dependents who have nothing to say in the management. The Church is not a huge industry: All members of the Church *are* Church, the Church belongs to all of them. And the shepherds are also *not* the *fathers* of the Church, in contrast to whom the laity are only minors who still cannot have any responsibility of their own for the Church. The Church cannot be considered simply as a family (except as under God, the one Father): All grown-up members of the Church are adult members who have an established inalienable responsibility for the whole. And, finally, the shepherds are also *not* the *teachers* of the Church, in contrast to whom the laity are only learning pupils who have only to listen and obey. The Church is not a school: All Church members have "learned from God" (1 Thess. 4:9) and "do not need anyone to teach" them (1 John 2:27).

In brief: In the Church, despite all the variations of office, which we must return to, all are ultimately equal insofar as they all are believers and, as such, adult brothers and sisters under the one Father and the one Lord Jesus. Teaching and advising, like listening and obeying, are, because all members are filled by the Spirit, *reciprocal*. To this extent the Church, despite all differences of services, is no two-class society of possessor and nonpossessor, empowered and powerless, adults and minors, knowledgeable and ignorant, but a community of love filled and authorized by the Spirit, in which only greater service bestows greater authority.

3. If then within this community of basic equality the variety of services and the special fullness of power of the pastoral office are nevertheless to be taken seriously, the question of the relation of the

Church (the local church or parish, the diocesan church, the universal Church) to the relevant pastoral office (pastor and his co-workers, bishop, pope) must be defined anew: Does the universal fullness of power of the Church confirm the particular fullness of power of the pastoral office, or is it the other way around—does the particular fullness of power of the pastoral office confirm the universal fullness of power of the Church? This must be examined carefully.

a. The joint decision-making of the laity in the Church can obviously *not be founded* on the fact that the fullness of power of the shepherds is derived simply from the fullness of power of the Church or congregation, from the fullness of power of the universal priesthood. Then the special pastoral office would simply be leveled within the Church and within the universal priesthood: an unbiblical democratization!

b. But on the other hand the participation of the laity in the decision-making of the Church can also *not* be *excluded* on the basis that the fullness of power of the Church or congregation is simply derived from the fullness of power of the shepherd, as though the shepherds alone stood in succession to the apostles and were not the servants of the Church but its masters or mediators. Thus the pastoral service would be isolated from the Church or congregation, from the universal priesthood, and its apostolic succession would be absolutized: an unbiblical hierarchicalization or clericalization of the Church!

c. If, however, as we saw, the Church and her shepherds stand all together under the one Father and Lord, who makes them all brothers; if they all stand under the one message of Christ and all are called into the same discipleship and the same obedience to God and his Word; if they then ultimately all are the hearing Church and precisely as hearers are all filled with the Spirit, then it follows that the fullness of power of the Church or congregation is not derived from the fullness of power of the shepherds, and the fullness of power of the shepherds is not derived from the fullness of power of Church or congregation, but the fullness of power of *both* is directly derived from the fullness of power of the Lord of the Church in his Spirit. This common origin of their fullness of power establishes the universal authorization of the congregation as well as the special fullness of power of the service of the shepherds. It is the support of the author-

Participation of the Laity 141

ity of the shepherds as well as of the participation of the "laity" in decision-making.

4. The joint decision-making of the "laity" in the Church will, then, be seen correctly only if Church or congregation and the shepherds are seen as intimately related as well as different. It is this perspective which eliminates all absolutistic decision-making by either the shepherds *or* the congregation alone, which excludes both ecclesiastical oligarchy (monarchy) *and* ochlocracy. If, as we have emphasized, the universal priesthood, if the various charismatic gifts and offices, and if especially the charismata of the prophets and teachers are taken seriously in the Church, then the *special office of the shepherds* (presiding officers) in the Church must and will also be taken very seriously: It is the special vocation of individual believing persons (in principle—for there is no biblical or dogmatic objection to it—both men and women) to the permanent and regular (not only occasional), public (not only private) service to the congregation as such (and not only to individual members) through the laying on of hands or ordination (and not only through the equally possible charism of the Spirit breaking through as he wills).

From this *special* service the shepherds have also *special* authority which can never be simply eliminated or passed over in the Church or congregation. From this special *service,* however, they have their authority only within, for, and in collaboration with the Church or congregation. So the *shepherds from the very outset are oriented to the joint collaboration, decision-making, and regulating of the congregation.* This orientation does not mean a constraint and restriction but a protection against all stifling isolation, a help in all their need, a liberation into true togetherness. The shepherds must see their special fullness of power embedded and protected in the universal authorization of the Church and of each individual church member. Solitary responsibility stifles, common responsibility sustains.

The word, baptism, the eucharist, forgiveness, the office of love are given to the entire Church. But a few must discharge the service of the word, the sacrament, and the Church permanently, regularly, and publicly in the Church, strengthened and legitimized for this through prayer and the power of ordination, which itself should occur in co-operation with the entire Church. Concretely: *All* Christians are empowered to preach the Word and to witness to the faith in the Church and in the world; but only to the shepherds of the congregation who are called, or to those delegated by them, is the special fullness of power to preach in the congregational assembly given. *All* Christians are empowered to exhort men to forgive their brother in a crisis of conscience; but only to the called shepherds is given the special fullness of power of the words of reconciliation and absolution, which is exercised in the congregational assembly upon the congregation and thus upon the individuals. For the coexecution of baptism and the eucharist *all* Christians are authorized; but only to the called shepherds is given the special fullness of power to perform baptisms in public in the congregation and to conduct responsibly the congregational eucharist.

5. Thus of their innermost essence the Church or congregation and the shepherds are oriented towards one another in decision-making. On the basis of his special mission with which he steps before the congregation, the ordained shepherd has a pregiven authority in the Church or the congregation. On the basis of his ordination the shepherd need not demonstrate his vocation, like every other charismatic, by the exhibition of his charism (in proof of the Spirit and the power). Rather he is appointed from the very beginning: legitimized as the one who is fully authorized for this office in a special way for the public activity of the congregation in the Spirit. But this must not be misunderstood, as though the shepherd ultimately were raised over the congregation to become the lord of the congregation, where he no longer remained dependent on the congregation. Every time a shepherd plays up his own person, every time he thinks and acts autocratically, conducts himself tyrannically and autonomously, he betrays the mission which he has received. He is not understanding that his special mission is a charism, a call from the Spirit to gain which he can do nothing, which has been given him without his earning it. He is wandering astray from the gospel which he has been called to serve and which demands of him that he serve men. All this would be an error and a fault in him, and the congregation and each Christian would be justified and called upon by the Spirit to show his opposition through open witness, provided he acted in truth and love. If however the special mission of the shepherd is received in faith, embraced each day with new fidelity, and exercised in love, then it must also give to the man sent the certainty that he has been truly sent with authority, the confidence that he can measure up to the call despite all personal weakness, the courage to attack the task anew again and again and to proclaim the word of God whether it is op-

portune or inopportune, the inner calm, despite all temptations, to endure to the end all crises and all assaults: "That is why I am reminding you now to fan into a flame the gift [charisma] that God gave you when I laid my hands on you. God's gift was not a spirit of timidity, but the Spirit of power, and love, and self-control. So you are never to be ashamed of witnessing to the Lord . . ." (2 Tim. 1:6–8).

So the shepherd and the congregation have their mutual obligations: The shepherd has the duty and the task to proclaim the Christian message to the congregation again and again, even when it is uncomfortable for the congregation. The congregation, on the other hand, has the duty and the task of retesting again and again whether the shepherd is remaining true to his commission, whether he is acting according to the gospel. For there are not only false prophets but also faithless shepherds. And if the Pauline statement "Never try to suppress the Spirit or treat the gift of prophecy with contempt" (1 Thess. 5:19–20) holds true especially for the presiding officers, then what follows certainly holds true not only for some presiding officers but for the entire congregation and each individual—"Think before you do anything—hold on to what is good and avoid every form of evil" (1 Thess. 5:21–22).

Thus everyone is helped by this mutual respectful examination, this reciprocal criticism without disputation, this universal *correctio fraterna* in modesty. And all this is a presupposition for common action, for which all that we have said is basically true: No individual decisions, either of the Church or congregation or of the shepherd! No going-it-alone, either of the "laity" without the shepherd or of the shepherd without the "laity." No sole control, either dictatorship of the one or dictatorship of the many! Instead of seclusion and isolation, openness and solidarity. Instead of paternalism, brotherliness. Instead of autocracy and despotism, service and love. Instead of servitude, freedom; instead of egotistic power, existence for others.[9]

6. If common responsibility, if joint decision-making of the congregation with the shepherd is seen in this way, then one need have no anxiety for the order of the congregation, even if it is threatened again and again from all sides. Then a first principle will be true for the shepherd as well as for the members of the congregation: *To each his own!* Then the shepherd will not assume a superiority over the congregation nor the congregation over the shepherd. Then neither shepherd nor laity will wish to commandeer and subordinate ev-

erything for themselves but they will each give and relinquish what belongs to the other. And then a second principle is valid: *With one another for one another!* Then neither the shepherd nor the laity will use their fullness of power as a weapon against the other in order to grasp a position for themselves and seize the power in the Church, but they will use this fullness of power, in the only way it makes sense, to serve one another and the whole. And finally there is one supreme criterion: *Obedience to the Lord!* Then neither the shepherd nor the laity will play the role of Lord of the Church, but they will find true freedom, imperturbable peace, and a permanent joy even amid difficulties and affliction in subordination to the one Lord and his word in love.

In this way a correct perspective on *obedience* in the Church is also possible. For Paul, the service which is actually occurring is the reason why subordination to those who make great exertions is obligatory. He who always volunteers for a special service—not only that of the shepherd but also of the prophet or teacher or helper etc. —and proves himself in it, he has the call of God, he has received the gift of grace of the Spirit. It is not simply a certain station, not a special tradition, not great age, not a long membership in the congregation, not even finally a conferring of the Spirit, but service itself perfected in the Spirit which creates authority in the congregation. Thus the obedience of everyone to God, Christ, the Spirit is demanded: Here *unconditional* obedience is valid. But toward men, whose will after all is certainly not always in accord with the will of God, there is even in the Church only a *conditional* and never a unilateral obedience. Free reciprocal subordination, free service of all for all, free obedience toward which the always-other gifts of grace of the other, is the consequence of obedience of all to God, Christ, the Spirit. The one Lord acts in one Spirit not through the shepherds but through all the various gifts of grace (1 Cor. 12:4–6). And the whole life of the Church will thus be a united living ensemble of shepherds and congregation, including all the various spiritual gifts and offices, amid which order and peace should rule—and yet the Spirit must never be muffled.

C. Embodiment

The embodiment of an ecclesiastical order which is justified by the original Christian message and Church must be different for different

times and different places. In every case a transposition is necessary.
Thus it is far from our intention to deliver a hard unhistorical judgment on times in which this ecclesiastical order was realized only
very imperfectly.[10] And likewise it is not our intention to give a
simple prescription or a universal remedy for a better realization
of such a truly Christian order to all the varied areas of the Church.
Nevertheless attention ought to be called to a few points of a general
nature.

Precisely what are the concrete possibilities for the participation of
the laity in the decision-making of the Church? Yves Congar has
called attention to the most important in the above-mentioned
book:[11]

1. the role of the laity in elections, and the occupying of ecclesiastical offices;

2. the role of the laity in councils;

3. the role of the princes in the Church;

4. the role of the congregation in the ordering of their own life
through the law of use and custom;

5. the participation of the laity in the administration of church
property and in ecclesiastical jurisdiction.

The role of the laity in the Council we have treated in detail on another occasion.[12] In view of the contemporary postconciliar situation,
continuing Congar's thought and at the same time following certain
items in the Council documents themselves, we can mention two
ways in which the participation of the laity in decision-making can be
concretized: first in the collegial church leadership on the various
levels and then also in the free election of presiding officers through
a representation of the pertinent churches.[13]

1. *The collegial church leadership on the various levels:*

The "collegiality" emphasized by the Council, that is the broth-
erly-communal character of church leadership, must not arbitrarily
remain limited to the uppermost level of the universal Church
(pope–bishops). It must also be realized on the level of the national
Church, the diocesan Church and above all the local church (and
correspondingly also in the religious orders with their lay brothers).
That means very clearly a dissolution of that authoritarian one-man
rule—whether on the level of the parish, bishopric, nation, or the
universal Church—which, as we have seen, is consonant neither with
the original New Testament organization nor with contemporary
democratic thought.

According to what we have already said about the shepherds, it is quite clear that the decisive authority of the pastor, the bishop, and the pope should remain explicitly preserved; only in this way can the mutual paralysis of the various powers normally be avoided. Nevertheless at the same time not only collaboration and counseling but also participation in decision-making by representative councils of the churches in question should be guaranteed. In order that these councils be truly representative it is necessary that the greater part of the members be elected in free and secret elections; a minority can be members ex officio because of certain important service functions or through their nomination by responsible shepherds (pastor, bishop, bishops' conference, or pope).

The constitutional foundations for these pressing and incisive reforms are laid down, at least for the diocese, by the Council itself: It was resolved by Vatican II that in every diocese a diocesan pastoral council should be established, to be composed of priests, religious, and laity. This pastoral council is already a reality in some dioceses, wherein the priests' council, also decreed by the Council, is partly integrated into this pastoral council, and the laity often have a two-thirds majority. In the concrete statutes of the diocesan council, care must be taken to assure that a true participation in decision-making is guaranteed, in which a kind of veto power (or a necessity of agreement) can be vested in the authorized shepherd. An appearance of collegiality which admits no true participation of the council in decision-making can do more harm than good; it is nothing but the collegial cloak for the old princely absolutism. Thus—a warning example to other levels—it was depressing to see how already at the first episcopal synod in Rome after the Council, true collegiality was completely overruled by the old papal absolutism: The things to be settled were unilaterally established and narrowed by the curial side; the most pressing problems of the universal Church (like regulation of births and celibacy) could not be discussed, no experts were admitted, much was discussed and resolved but nothing was decided; the bishops traveled home without knowing which of these agreements the pope and the curial apparatus would bring to realization; practically speaking, the bishops' synod had no serious immediate effects.

Analogous to the diocesan level, collegial leadership of the Church must also be realized on the other levels:

a. For the universal Church it would mean to constitute a lay council parallel to the bishops' council which is already constituted, though still not permanent, still not assembling regularly, and still possessing no authority. This could come about as a result of the international lay congress, which in the postconciliar period showed more vitality, courage, and resolution than the synod of bishops. This lay council, together with the bishops' council under the decisive leadership of the pope (the veto power), could not only give advice but also decide on the important concerns of the universal Church.

b. For each nation there should be constituted, again paralleling the diocesan pastoral council, a national pastoral council, consisting of bishops, priests and laity, for counseling and communal decision-making in all important concerns of the national Church.

c. For every parish there should be constituted, where this has not already happened, a parish council of men and women, paralleling the diocesan pastoral council, for the purposes of counseling and participation in decision-making with the pastor (who would have veto power) in all important parish concerns.

For the concrete statute the following should be observed:

a. In all the decision-making councils we have described, from the parish council to the lay senate and the bishops' council of the entire Church, it should be self-explanatory that a sufficient number of qualified *women* are also to be admitted as members. Such representation is a part of the full participation of women in the life of the Church on the basis of equality. On the various levels care must be taken eventually for the education and inclusion of women in active coresponsibility.

b. On every level theological and other *professional people* are to be drawn in, corresponding to the scholarly areas under discussion.

c. For practical functioning the American principle of "checks and balances," which precludes a monopolization of power in certain hands, is helpful. In the United States the president as well as Congress has a strong post. And so ultimately the president can do nothing without Congress, and Congress can do nothing without the president. The executive branch (the president) can employ a strong initiative and in emergency even a strong brake. But it is bound by the resolutions of the legislative branch (Congress), against which the president can—but in practice seldom does—apply a veto. Moreover, both the president and Congress are controlled by the judiciary branch (the courts). So the president and Congress mutually hinder and help one another. Autocracy and the dictatorship of an individual is avoided, just as is ochlocracy and the fragmentation of the many, all of which benefits both the freedom of the individual and the well-being of the whole.[14]

2. *Free election of presiding officers through a representation of the pertinent churches:*

This should hold true for pastors, bishops, and pope. Such an election can be arranged with the co-operation of the representative councils discussed above, to which, circumstances permitting, other members can be co-opted for the electoral college: For the election of the pope in the universal Church the bishops' council and lay council would be duly qualified, for the election of the bishop in the diocese the diocesan pastoral council, for the election of the pastor in the local church the parish council (or, as in some Swiss cantons, the assembled congregation).

In the election of the pastor and bishops a control function would belong to the superior pastoral offices: The election of pastors would have to be approved by the bishops, the election of bishops by the episcopal conference in its majority or by the pope. In this way the old axioms of canon law would once again hold good and could be applied by analogy to all ecclesiastical offices: "No bishop should be installed against the will of the people" (Pope Celestine I) and "He who presides over all should be elected by all" (Pope Leo the Great).

As to concrete regulations, several points would be important:

a. Election not only of the superiors of religious orders, or, as in certain church areas, the pastor, but also of the bishops and all office-holders for a substantial but stipulated time (e.g., six or eight years with the possibility of re-election) is a justified as well as a pressing desideratum in today's situation.

b. Directives for obligatory (e.g., at seventy years) or optional (e.g., at sixty-five years) resignation from ecclesiastical offices are necessary. On the other side, demands of a congregation for the retirement of a shepherd should never be legally binding without the agreement of the superior office-holder (bishop for the pastor, pope or episcopal conference for the bishop); in this way illegitimate attempts at pressure can be averted from the pertinent administrator.

c. A special committee should advise the bishop in all personnel concerns; such a group can consider each case carefully—the special peculiarities and requisites of the position concerned as well as the wishes of the congregation and of the person in question. Special attention must be given to the pastor-assistant relationship, which is full of vexation.

Only one example, though one which has central significance, shall be investigated here more closely: election of bishops.[15] The election of the bishop of Rome, the pope, will not be treated specially here; nevertheless it must be clear even without a long explanation how pressing the transferral of the election from the college of cardinals, which is in no way representative and in any case is anachronistic, to the episcopal and lay councils is: Today more than ever the pope needs the broadest consensus in the Church!

The election of the bishop by a representative council of the pertinent church satisfies the following:

1. the theological as well as practical high esteem for the particular and local church, for the diocese and the congregation (cf. esp. the Constitution on the Church, Art. 26, and the Constitution on the Bishops, e.g., Art. 27);

2. the demand for decentralization, which stipulates a dismantling of the power of the Roman Curia in favor of the churches in the individual nations (establishment of national bishops conferences, etc.; cf. Decree on the Bishops, e.g., Arts. 36–38);

3. the demand for a curial reform (which, unfortunately, has still not been radically accomplished), which will provide not a broadening of the area of curial competence over against the episcopates of individual countries, but on the contrary the insertion of representatives of the most varied countries into the ecclesiastical central administration (cf. Constitution on the Bishops, Arts. 9–10);

4. the strict definition (which here would mean limitation) of the authority of the nuncio, as desired by the Council: "The Fathers also eagerly desire that, in view of the pastoral role proper to bishops, the office of legates of the Roman Pontiff be more precisely determined" (Decree on the Bishops' Pastoral Office in the Church, Art. 9; cf. Art. 10).

For a historical understanding of these conclusions of Vatican II it must be remembered that these conclusions doubtless stand in a clear front line against Roman centralism, dirigism, and absolutism, as it has prevailed in the West since the Gregorian reform and the High Middle Ages and reached its insurpassable high point in the period after Vatican I with the new codification of the Code of Canon Law. But on the basis of what has been stated here from the New Testament, it must be clear that these conclusions are not concerned with attempted "innovations," but with a return to tradition,[16] the truly good old tradition. The election of bishops is itself an excellent model for this, as it was earlier. In the election of bishops it was from the beginning kept in mind that not only a clerical hierarchy of functionaries but rather the entire community of believers, the entire People of God, is the Church. In ancient Christian times the bishop was *elected by clergy and people,* even if he then was ordained generally by the neighboring bishops. Some of the greatest bishops of all times like Ambrose of Milan and Augustine of Hippo were elected decisively by the people. "Nos eligimus eum," "We elect him"—ran the formula of acclamation of the people in the Latin congregations. Not the Roman bishop but the neighboring bishops authoritatively co-operated in the election. The right of corroboration and consecration also belonged later, according to the stipulations of the First Ecumenical Council of Nicaea, not to the Roman See but to the metropolitan of the ecclesiastical province involved. How the nomination to the episcopal sees passed in later times in part to the princes, and how the biblically based right of the people of the Church was more and more limited cannot be treated here in detail. In any case the reform movement of the Middle Ages still demanded the free election of bishops by clergy and people (so decreed Leo IX at the Synod of Rheims in 1049). The free episcopal election as over against nomination by the princes succeeded in principle in the battle over investiture. Indeed because of the growing predominance of the cathedral chapter, the lower clergy and the laity were more and more excluded from the election. At first the cathedral chapter had only to assent to an election; then more and more it could determine the election. The election right of the cathedral chapter became common toward the end of the twelfth century and was established as obligatory by Innocence III for the entire Church.

Through this development, favored by the popes, the right of corroboration and ordination more and more fell to the Roman see, although in the early centuries the influence of the Roman bishop in reference to episcopal elections did not extend essentially beyond his metropolitan (or patriarchal) right, and only after the ninth century in case of complications (removal, promotion, election controversies) did he regularly interfere in the filling of a vacancy. After the High Middle Ages the right of corroboration was often used for the purpose of exerting influence on the election itself. This eventuated in the reservations by which the popes withheld to themselves the filling of episcopal seats: first of all for isolated cases, then for certain seats, finally after the fourteenth century (under the Avignon pope Urban V, in 1363) in general. Thus the suffrage of the chapter was undermined and in time even legally suppressed. Only after the Western Schism and in the struggle over the Council of Basel was an at least circumscribed episcopal suffrage of the cathedral chapter again recognized through the Viennese Concordat of 1448. Indeed it came about in the aftermath of the development of a royal or noble right of nomination which took many forms (in some cases the right of lesser acceptability: *personae minus gratae*). With the abolition of the Catholic ruling houses these rights declined vastly. In this manner the way was first cleared for a general papal naming of bishops, which had already long been in the making and now was established in proper form in the new Codex Juris Canonici, which was proclaimed by Rome in 1918 without any essential participation of the episcopacy and amid the complete exclusion of the universal Church. The chiefly unrestricted right to elect bishops in the Swiss bishoprics of Basel, Chur, and St. Gall as well as of Olmütz remain now the great exceptions. Only in the Eastern Churches united to Rome has the right of nomination formed in the ancient Church era to an extent remained preserved, and the new law of the Eastern Churches recently accepted the rule that the bishop be elected by the synod of bishops of the patriarchs. Yet this freedom of election is diluted insofar as the list of candidates must be approved by Rome in advance! The spirit of the resolutions of Vatican II means a reinclusion of clergy and laity in the election of bishops after the model of the ancient Church.[17]

In conclusion let us say only this: Obviously there is no perfect system of organization; in concrete life each has its specific defects and dangers. But a system better than that canonized by the present Code of Canon Law is not difficult to think of![18] The one suggested here in some of its basic features corresponds better both to the original organization of the apostolic Church and to our contemporary democratic times.

Translated by ARLENE SWIDLER

NOTES

1. Yves Congar, *Jalons pour une théologie du laïcat* (Paris, 1953); *Lay People in the Church* (Westminster, Md., 1957).
2. Cf. the very helpful article by F. Klostermann, "Allgemeine Pastoraltheologie der Gemeinde," in *Handbuch der Pastoraltheologie* III (Freiburg, Basel, Vienna, 1968), p. 43: "For this reason there also exists that fundamental collegiality and conciliarity in the congregation, the community of Christ, of which we have already spoken. Therefore no one in the Church is only a presiding officer and no one is only a subordinate. Therefore behind and before every special calling in the community there is a common, basic Christian calling and a common, basic Christian status, in which everyone is reverend, excellent and eminent, in which everyone is spiritual (Rom. 8) and everyone 'ecclesiastical,' even if the current ecclesiastical law book still always speaks with predilection of clerics as 'ecclesiastici.' Therefore in the Church there must be brotherliness, conversation, joint responsibility of all for all, partnership and dialogue. Consequently even the highest hierarchs are never simply vis-à-vis the community, but at the same time are always fellow Christians, fellow students, fellow servants, as Augustine said, to whom still another service has been entrusted, as a different one has to another person, without, nevertheless, their losing all their fundamental equality."
3. F. Klostermann, *Das Zweite Vatikanische Konzil. Konstitutionen, Dekrete und Erklärungen* (Freiburg/Basel/Vienna, 1966/67), I, 260–83; II, 585–701.
4. Cf. the recent article by E. Golomb, "Kirchenstruktur Brüderlichkeit," *Wort und Wahrheit* 23 (1968), 291–305.
5. What N. Greinacher says in "Der Vollzug der Kirche im Bistum," in *Handbuch der Pastoraltheologie* III (Freiburg/Basel/Vienna, 1968), p. 106, concerning the diocese is valid also for the parish and the universal Church: "There often still stands in the way of the realization of brotherliness and collegiality in the diocese a *paternalism* that is profoundly unchristian. For God himself has made an end to paternity on earth—there may yet be a physical vicarious kind—as his Son entered as our brother into humanity and its history. It is time therefore to make an end to a paternalism that is socially obsolete as well as essentially unchristian. Brotherliness and paternalism in the Church are mutually exclusive. The very difficult question arises of whether Christian brotherliness does not slide into the background in the Church to the same degree as the notion of the father in reference to the pope, bishops, and priests pushes to the fore. W. Dirks is correct in saying, 'If the Evangelical Church is threatened more by excessive fraternal confusion, in the Catholic Church it is the Father image, the fear of brotherhood, which threatens the Word of Christ in history.' "
6. Cf. the very illuminating article by J. Neumann, "Das 'jus divinum' im Kirchenrecht," in *Orientierung* 31 (1967), 5–8.

7. On apostolic succession cf. besides the usual works on the Church in the New Testament (by O. Linton and F. M. Braun, and the monographs by F. J. Leenhardt, N. A. Dahl, O. Michel, G. Johnston, W. Robinson, A. Oepke, G. Aulén, L. G. Champion, A. Nygren, P. Minear, K. H. Schelkle, R. Schnackenburg, L. Cervaux) the more specialized researches by Ph. H. Menoud, *L'Eglise et le ministère selon le Nouveau Testament* (Neuchâtel, 1949); G. W. H. Lampe, *Some Aspects of the New Testament Ministry* (London, 1949); H. von Campenhausen, *Kirchliches Amt und geistliche Vollmacht in den ersten drei Jahrhunderten* (Tübingen, 1953); H. Schlier, *Die Zeit der Kirche* (Freiburg im Breisgau, 1955), 129–47; G. Dix, *Le Ministère dans l'église ancienne* (Neuchâtel/Paris, 1955); E. Schweizer, *Gemeinde und Gemeindeordnung im Neuen Testament* (Zurich, 1959); E. Käsémann, *Exegetische Versuche und Besinnungen* I (Göttingen, 1960), 109–34; H. U. von Balthasar, *Sponsa Verbi* (Einsiedeln, 1960), 80–147; E. Schlink, *Der kommende Christus und die kirchlichen Traditionen* (Göttingen, 1961), 160–95; for literature from the fields of history and systematic theology on the subject of ecclesiastical office, see H. Küng, *Structures of the Church* (New York, 1964), chapter VI (includes a response to the positions of Käsemann and Schlink), and the pertinent lexicon articles.

8. For the basic foundation of all that follows see H. Küng, *The Church* (New York, 1968), chapter E.

9. Cf. Greinacher, p. 106 f.: "If we are in earnest when we speak of Christian brotherliness and the equality of the members of the diocese, we must move toward a far-reaching *democratization of the structures of the Church.* Such a democratization corresponds on the one hand to an original and genuine stream of Christian tradition in the Church and on the other hand also to the mentality and the structures of contemporary secular society, which, as we have shown, cannot conceal its own Christian origins. One thing must be clear: one cannot speak of the co-responsibility of the laity if participation in *decision-making* is not granted. The summons of the laity to co-responsibility and care for the diocese has meaning really only if this laity is also guaranteed a genuine role in diocesan decision-making. If this is not the case, then one not unjustly runs the danger that this summons to joint care will be regarded as a farce. If the complaint is heard so often that the laity show so slight an interest in the call to participation in the apostolate, then it should be asked whether the necessary place has also been made for their role in decision-making. Only under this condition of genuine participation in decision-making will it be possible in the long run to integrate the laity into the Church in any authentic way."

10. Peter Stockmeier, "Gemeinde und Bischofsamt in der alten Kirche," *Theologische Quartalschrift* (Tübingen), vol. 149, no. 2 (1969), 133–46, shows of course that the constitution of the ancient Church was very much closer, and not only just in time, to the original Christian message and Church than is the constitution of the post-Tridentine Church.

11. Congar, 329–33.

12. Küng, *Structures of the Church,* chapter V.

13. The notions raised here are developed in a more general context in Küng's *Truthfulness: The Future of the Church* (New York, 1968), chapter B, IX.

14. Further possibilities of co-operation between presiding officers and congregation are discussed by A. Müller and R. Völkel, "Die Funktion der Laien in der Pfarrgemeinde," in *Handbuch für Pastoraltheologie* III (Freiburg/Basel/Vienna, 1968), 233–53.

15. On the election of bishops cf. besides the manuals on the history of canon law (especially E. Feine, Wm. Plöchl), the short summary by K. Mörsdorf in the article "Bischof III. Kirchenrechtlich," in *Lexikon für Theologie und Kirche* II (Freiburg im Breisgau, 1958), 497–505; Günter Biemer, "Die Bischofswahl als neues Desiderat kirchlicher Praxis," *Theologische Quartalschrift,* vol. 149, no. 2 (1969), 171–84; Johannes Neumann, "Wahl und Amtszeitbegrenzung nach kanonischem Recht," *ibid.,* 117–32; Stockmeier, *op. cit.*

16. Cf. esp. Stockmeier, *op. cit.*

17. Greinacher, p. 107: "If it is correct that every believing Christian is a brother or sister of Jesus and that the Spirit of Christ operates in each, that the Spirit blows where it will, and that there is also charisma outside office, then the idea cannot be excluded that these Christians should also exert an influence on the fulfillment of the Church in the diocese and on the *filling of posts of service.* In the election of the apostle Matthias (Acts 1:15–26) as well as in the election of deacons (Acts 6:1–6), the collaboration of the entire community was considered self-explanatory (cf. also Acts 15:22 f.). It is well-known that the leaders of the congregations in the first centuries up to the time of Ambrose and Augustine were determined with the collaboration of the congregation. Until recently the Church tolerated a situation in which the nobility exerted an influence on the filling of certain parish positions. Even up to the year 1903 the Church countenanced the fact that in practice the Kaiser influenced the papal elections. Up until our own time— and not only in Eastern countries—the governments in some countries exerted a massive influence on the episcopal elections. Would it not be more appropriate to give some influence in the filling of offices to everyone who is immediately concerned and who is coresponsible for the bishopric —namely, the members of the local church? Is it not time to give the old democratic tendencies in the Church another chance and endow them with a new meaning and a new expression which would be suitable for our time, which is characterized by the process of 'fundamental democratization'?"

18. Cf. esp. Biemer, *op. cit.* and Neumann, "Wahl und Amtszeitbegrenzung nach kanonischem Recht."

vague outline, has been largely robbed of her sexuality. For a long time she has been absolutized as Christianity's only important female figure and has been placed on a par with Christ. Such a cultic veneration of Mary has not, however, affected the estimation of women in the social realm. What is more, as a result, the multiplicity of female figures mentioned in the Bible (from judge and prophetess Deborah and the young woman in the Song of Songs to church leaders Phoebe and the missionary Prisca) have been neglected. Only a Mariology which does not avoid a historical analysis of her virginity and accepts Mary as a complete woman, instead of simply as an exemplary humble handmaid, can help people of today to a better understanding of the Christian message.

B. Women in Society

4. The subordination of the wife is not intrinsic to a Christian marriage. New Testament statements concerning the subordination of a wife to her husband (mostly found in later New Testament writings) must be understood in their sociocultural context and present sociocultural conditions must be taken into account. Many married couples of today have discovered that a marriage based on equality is in greater accord with the dignity of human beings who, as man and woman, have both been created in the image of God.

5. Nor can one deduce from the essence of a Christian marriage a specific division of labor—for instance, that the woman is to raise the children, while the man is to be the breadwinner. Raising children and doing housework, as well as financially supporting the family, can be performed by wife and husband together.

6. Parents should, therefore, encourage their daughters no less than their sons to get a good academic education or vocational training. By the same token, sons should be trained for future parental and household duties. To be sure, "working woman" is not identical with "liberated woman," but neither should the opportunities of women be seen exclusively in the alternatives married and housewife or unmarried and religious. In raising one's children, in sermons, religion class, and marital counseling, the multiplicity of occupational opportunities and roles for women should be emphasized.

3. Women in Church and Society

A. Fundamental Theological Ideas

1. Beginning with the concept of God, an overemphasis on masculinity must be avoided. God cannot be claimed exclusively for the male sex. "God" is not identical with "man"; in the Old Testament God also has feminine, motherly traits. Calling God "Father" must not signify a sexual differentiation in the deity Itself. God as "Father" is a patriarchal symbol, an analogue for the transhuman, transsexual reality of God, who is also the origin of all that is feminine and motherly. In no case should this symbol be used as a religious justification for a patriarchal social system.

2. The animosity and even hostility of many Church Fathers and subsequent theologians toward women does not reflect the attitude of Jesus but rather the attitude of numerous male contemporaries of Jesus, who thought women were socially insignificant and believed they should avoid the company of men in public. The Gospels, however, in the historical biographical details, do not hesitate to speak of Jesus' relations with women. According to Gospel accounts, Jesus disregarded the custom of excluding women from public life. He displayed not only a lack of contempt for women but also a remarkable openness toward them: from the very beginning, women belonged to the special followers of Jesus, who supported him and accompanied him and the twelve disciples from Galilee to Jerusalem. Personal attachment to women was not alien to Jesus; women witnessed his death and burial. When he forbade husbands, who were the only ones allowed to draw up a letter of divorce, to divorce their wives, Jesus raised the human and juridical status of women in his society considerably. Therefore, no Christology may emphasize Jesus' masculinity more than his humanity (as the title "Son of God" seems to do). God's revelation did not occur specifically through a man but rather through a human being.

3. In a Mariology formulated by celibate men, Mary, the mother of Jesus, a figure whom we can historically comprehend only in

7. Birth control, if practiced responsibly and not abused to exploit the woman (the sexual revolution is not to be equated with women's liberation!), can contribute to the genuine liberation of women by making it possible for them to complete their education, better co-ordinate career and family life and—especially where lower-class women are concerned—reduce their financial burden and workload.

8. In the controversial issue of abortion one must take into account not only the rights of the fetus but also the physical and mental health of the woman, her social situation, and her family responsibilities, particularly in relation to existing children who must be provided and cared for.

C. Women in the Church

9. In order that the Catholic Church, whose power structure and ministry are completely dominated by men, might become a Church of all human beings, women should be represented in all decision-making bodies and at all levels—the parish, diocesan, national, and international. A blatant example of women's nonrepresentation is the Vatican Congregations for Religious. Not one single woman is a member of this body. Further, according to present legislation, only men can be voting members of an ecumenical council, and only men can elect a pope. These are questions of human, not divine, law.

10. Since liturgical language should express the fact that the congregation is composed of both women and men who have equal rights, one should never address the "brothers" or the "sons of God" only, but also the "sisters" and "daughters of God," or both together as "children of God." Rather than speaking of Christ redeeming "men" or "mankind," one can say "people" or "humanity."

11. Women should be encouraged to study theology. In order that the Church and theology (ethics, and in particular sexual ethics) profit in all aspects from the insights of women, they should be admitted to all degree programs in theology (including those at Catholic seminaries)—in many places they are still admitted only under certain conditions or not at all—and should be supported by church institutions no less than male theology students (through church scholarships, the subsidizing of scholarly works, etc.).

12. Members of women's religious orders that have often been highly effective in realizing Vatican II's principles of reform are often more hindered than helped by the male official church. In spite of the lack of priests, they are seldom allowed to take over leadership functions in congregations, and, although church funds are amply bestowed upon candidates for the priesthood, they are often denied the financial means to an adequate education. A remedy is urgently needed, especially in view of the rapidly shrinking numbers of women entering religious orders.

13. The forced celibacy of priests often leads to an unnaturally tense relationship between priests and women, in which women are frequently viewed as sexual beings only and a sexual temptation. Thus there is a connection between the prohibition of marriage for ordained men and the prohibition of ordination for women; women will not be ordained and will not be fully accepted as colleagues in the administrative and decision-making bodies of the Church until clerical celibacy is replaced by a celibacy freely chosen by those truly called to it.

14. The reintroduction of the diaconate of women, which was first abolished by the Western Church and then died out in the Eastern Church, would be a desirable reform. But if the admission of women to the diaconate is not accompanied by their admission to the presbyterate, this measure instead of leading to equality, will just delay the ordination of women. Further, those Catholic parishes which now allow women to assume some liturgical functions (conducting Mass, serving as lay readers, distributing communion, giving the sermon) are to be highly commended. But while this can be an important step toward the full integration of women into church leadership, it, too, does not render superfluous the full ordination of women.

15. There are no serious theological reasons opposing the presbyterate of women. That the council of the Twelve was exclusively male must be understood in light of the sociocultural situation of the time. The reasons for the exclusion of women offered by tradition (through woman sin entered the world; woman was created second; woman was not made in the image of God; women are not full members of the Church; menstruation makes woman impure) cannot call on Jesus as their witness, and are evidence of a fundamental the-

ological defamation of women. In view of the leadership of women in the early Church (Phoebe, Prisca) and in view of the completely changed status of today's women in the economic system, in academia, state, and society, the admission of women to the presbyterate should be delayed no longer. Jesus and the early Church were ahead of their time in their estimation of women; today's Catholic Church is far behind the times, and also far behind other Christian churches.

16. It would be a misunderstanding of ecumenism if the Catholic Church, referring to the reserve of more conservative "brother churches," were to delay long overdue reforms such as the ordination of women. Instead of using such churches as an alibi, they, in turn, should be challenged to reform. On this issue many Protestant churches could serve as a model for the Catholic Church.

For a long time both in theory and practice, the Catholic Church has discredited and defamed women and at the same time exploited them. Along with the dignity due them, it is time to guarantee women an appropriate juridical and social status.

Translated by FRANCIS X. MURPHY

V. Worship Today—Why?

Can We Speak to God?

The alternative

Some years ago Rudolf Augstein, editor of *Der Spiegel,* captured public attention with a theological book, *Jesus, Son of Man* [*Jesus Menschensohn*]. The theologians criticized this book from top to bottom—unfortunately, not without reason. The last chapter however deserves serious consideration. It represents the climax of the whole book: "Without him what is to be done?" What is to be done without Jesus Christ?

Augstein's clear alternative to Christian faith is: "There is no God whom we know or about whom we can speak" (p. 408). We must "live without religion" (p. 422). We are not spared the necessity "of leaning out into nothingness" (p. 423). Of course we have to "survive" (p. 423). But how? By "applying our reason to the thoroughly banal process of coping with life" (p. 425). We must simply attempt to "make the best we can of ourselves, our life and society . . . in meaningful work, meaningful joy, meaningful hate" (p. 425). "If we improve nothing, if we fail, then we are at least no worse off than before" (p. 426).

This then is the alternative to Christian belief in God. I respect it and I do not want to belittle any of it. Atheists often lead better lives than Christians. Nevertheless I must raise some questions:

Should we—even nonreligious parents often ask themselves this question—educate our children and the younger generation as a whole, without faith, for the rational, banal process of coping with life: without a final orientation, without deeper meaning, higher ideals, without great and living hope?

Should they then have no other support than themselves and their easily deceived, confused, seduced reason? Exposed to all the addictions, constraints, and ideologies of our time?

Can we then give them no answer to those questions of human life which cannot be suppressed simply by prohibiting them?

Where does man come from and where does he go to?

Why do what we do? Why is the world as it is?
Why are we here? What is it all about?
What then is the ultimate reason and meaning of all reality?
And what really holds for our action: Why and to whom are we ulti-
mately responsible? What deserves contempt and what love?
Why fight at all for justice and freedom?
What is the point of loyalty and friendship, but also what is the point
of suffering and guilt?
And finally what is there left for us: death, making everything point-
less at the end? What will give us courage to live and courage to die?

In all these questions it is all or nothing. They are questions not
for weaklings and uninformed people but precisely for the informed
and committed. They are not excuses for not acting but incentives to
action.

Is there something which sustains us in all this, which never permits us to despair?

Something stable in all change, something unconditioned and absolute in the relativizing experienced everywhere?

And what is the character of this ultimate reality? good or evil?
indifferent or friendly to men? Incomprehensible, without any quali-
ties, or perhaps even greater than all that can be conceived?

I think that Christian faith has answers to all these questions and
they are not cheap answers. There are of course cheap Christian answers. But today particularly, as Christians, we do not have to believe every absurdity. For there is a midway between unbelief and superstition.

It is that utterly reasonable and yet more than reasonable reliance
on an ultimate great mystery in our life which demands trust,
requires a commitment, and which at the same time makes it possible
both to stand still and to go forward.

Everyone believes in something. Rudolf Augstein believes in man's
reason. After many experiences of recent, very recent history, I prefer to believe in God: as a wholly rational human being, I think, to
believe in God.

Believing in God

There is an alternative to the unbelieving, purely rational, thoroughly banal affirmation of life which is once more being actively
propagated today. It is to believe in God and not in human reason,
but to do so as a wholly rational being.

What does this mean? It is true that we can no longer believe like ancient and medieval people in a God who dwells literally or spatially "above" the world, from whom the Son of God "descends" and to whom he again "ascends": These are images, profound images, symbols. Nor can we any longer believe in a God who dwells in the intellectual, metaphysical sense "outside" the world in an extramundane beyond and who only occasionally intervenes in this world.

No, a modern understanding of God must explain how God is *in* this world and this world in God:

a God who eludes our apprehension and comprehension as air or light elude us when we want to grasp them and who nevertheless is more real than all that is real: the ultimate reality in men's hearts and at the heart of things;

the infinite in all the finite, the constant in all the inconstant, the unconditioned, the absolute in all that is conditioned and relative;

the unfathomable, inscrutable primal reason, primal source, primal meaning of all that is. We must start out from this.

If then I had to say quite simply why we do not have to fear this primal reason, as a Christian, I would point to this Christ. In the man Jesus of Nazareth it has become unambiguously clear that this primal reason of the world and of man is not a dark and awful chasm but a superradiant, loving expanse of light, behind all the clouds, on whom we can absolutely rely on clear days or dark days, in living and dying.

God as he showed himself in Jesus is the guarantee, not only that all will be well at the end but that everything has meaning here and now:

that there is meaning in living, loving, acting, in committing ourselves to justice, freedom, human dignity;

that there is also meaning in despising some things and respecting others, in keeping faith, cultivating friendship, but also in forgiving sin and enduring suffering.

We should reflect more on what joy God means, could mean, for human life and remember that it was precisely this Jesus who made people aware of the fact. So we have every reason to be grateful.

Thanking

From time to time—and the act of worship provides an opportunity for this—we should at least take a couple of minutes to think of what lies behind us. There is much that we do not want to recall. But there is much that we simply cannot recall without giving thanks. For "thanking" and "thinking" are originally the same word.

What do I want to give thanks for?

Well, certainly for all that is taken for granted, but which so many cannot take for granted: for health, food and drink, clothes, holidays, so many joys. But also for all developments for the better in human society: progress in science and technology, social progress, improvement in international relations. . . .

But everyone has also quite personal reasons for gratitude. For instance, I wrote a dangerous theological book and I have come safely through another year; I went skiing and did not break my leg; I drove a car and was lucky.

And there are other small miracles:
colleagues who were never dishonest;
reconciliation after a serious quarrel;
friendship which has endured;
help when help seemed impossible;
a way out of a hopeless situation.

So then I would like to give thanks. To whom? Well, to *all* those to whom I owe so much.

Often, admittedly, it was sheer chance that all went well. But we cannot thank chance. As a believer, I would like to thank him who stands behind chance, who is at work in all things, to whom I owe myself.

You may perhaps ask: Can we speak to God? Is he a person? Well, certainly not a person like you and me: the primal reason and primal meaning of all reality is not an individual person alongside other persons. But God is certainly not less than a person. He is not impersonal.

Or could a God without mind and understanding be a God? Could such a God explain mind and understanding, freedom and love, in the world and in man? No, God is not below our level.

Even though we can speak of God only in analogical terms, in metaphors and images, nevertheless we can speak to him. From the first page to the last the Bible speaks of a genuine partner, who loves men and is absolutely reliable: not an object, not empty, unechoing space, not an anonymous interpersonal something, but a genuine Thou.

I want then to thank this God and trust myself to him continually for the future. Sometimes I find help in a prayer that a young Jew, if I remember rightly, wrote on the wall of the Warsaw ghetto, a very encouraging, cheering prayer:

I believe in the sun, even if it does not shine.
I believe in love, even if I do not feel it.
I believe in God, even if I do not see him.

In joy and pain, happiness and unhappiness, we may speak to God. This is man's great opportunity, a true grace, the grace of God himself. Here is the ground of all prayer and all worship.

But what does worship, religious service, mean? Is worship only for Sunday?

Worship in Ordinary Life

Paul writes to the community in Rome:

I exhort you therefore, brothers, by the mercy of God, to offer your bodies as a living sacrifice, holy and pleasing to God.
This is your spiritual service of God.
Do not be conformed to the structure of this world, but be transformed in a new mind, so as to be able to test what is God's will, that is what is good, pleasing, and perfect. [Rom. 12:1–2]

The Church today is not always a pleasant sight. But at least one aspect is pleasing. Both Catholics and Protestants have gained a new awareness of the fact that the Christian religious service cannot be restricted to congregational worship on Sundays. Their divine service is, should be, can be essentially service of God in the midst of the world, in the midst of human society, in the midst of their wholly personal daily life. Genuinely Christian worship consists in being a Christian in ordinary life. This is how the Christian praises and honors God.

This is just what is meant by these two programmatic statements placed as a leitmotif at the opening of the most detailed exhortation (parenesis) which the Apostle Paul ever wrote. In this letter to the community in Rome he appeals to God's mercy, not insisting on a burdensome duty or obligation but pointing to a great opportunity, a decisive possibility, a true grace for man. For Christian worship must be something quite different from the sacrifices which men have offered in the course of the history of religions from the most ancient times:

not a sacrifice of slaughtered animals or the offering of dead, material things but the living commitment of man himself, in unobtrusive service to his fellow men, sympathetic or unsympathetic, who are living with him and around him. This then is worship of God:

not only on certain holy days, Sundays, and feast days but on all days, on working days throughout the year;

not only at certain sacred places but in all places—even the most profane—in the world;

not only in the form of certain sacred actions but in man's whole life, work, struggle, suffering;

not offered only by certain sacred persons but by all kinds of believing Christians.

Worship therefore which is not—so to speak—interiorized as a private refinement of our personal existence but which is also a practical, public gesture on a large or small scale;

worship which is not only devout and edifying for the soul but for the whole man with flesh and blood, mind and body, brain and sexuality: "Offer your bodies as a living sacrifice, holy and pleasing to God."

It is clear that this is not what is usually described as "worship." But that very thing which appears to be completely secular, profane, is described by the apostle as "holy" and "pleasing to God": a "spiritual service" which is not tied to outward ceremonies, to particular times, places, or persons, but which takes place in the Spirit, in accordance with what John says, "in spirit and in truth" (John 4:23).

Worship on Sunday?

That much had to be said directly in the light of Paul's text. But I don't want to make it too easy for myself. Anyone in our churches today who wants to be open-minded and to speak frankly in a way suited to the times will also have to speak of the worldliness, secularity, profanity, and rationality of the Christian life. But, where so many are already loudly playing the same tune, we need not blow our own trumpet. Here we shall consider the facts and—in order not to be too boring—try to add a counterpoint.

It must be recognized that the situation today is completely dif-

ferent from that in which Paul made his statement. What Paul could
take for granted in his exhortation to offer God our service in
ordinary life has largely disappeared. He was writing to a congregation: quite concretely, to a congregational assembly where the letter was read aloud. Could Paul ever have imagined that he would
one day be writing for Christians most of whom no longer assemble
at all for a religious service, for prayers or the eucharist in the congregational gathering—even in a very secular place? I am not thinking simply of those Protestant churches which are almost empty on
Sundays. In West Germany attendance in the Catholic Church on
Sundays has also seriously declined: from 50.6 per cent in 1950 to
32.4 per cent in 1972. Against these reduced numbers in the
shrunken congregations must be set the figure of 84 per cent of
Christians in the same area who, according to a survey, did not want
to leave the Church. But what is particularly disturbing is the fact
—to which many pastors can testify—that young people between
sixteen and twenty-five scarcely count among churchgoers. In view
of these conditions, what will the situation be like in a few decades?

In the light of this alarming state of affairs in Protestantism and
Catholicism, unfortunately not only in Germany, I shall make bold
—and I am well aware of the risk involved—to speak now not about
worship in ordinary life but about worship on Sundays in church. Is
this permissible, particularly for a Catholic speaking in a Protestant
church? Certainly, according to Martin Luther. In his Larger Catechism he requires participation in Sunday worship precisely in the
name of the freedom of a Christian and vehemently attacks the in-
dolence of those "loathsome spirits . . . who, after hearing a sermon
or two, have had enough and more than enough, and think they can
get on very well by themselves and have no need of a master" (third
commandment): merely "celebrating and being idle" does not make
a "christian's feast day"; non-Christians could do as much. Similarly, according to the Reformed Heidelberg Catechism, "particularly
on feast days God's congregation should come diligently to learn the
word of God, to make use of the holy sacraments, publicly to invoke
the Lord and to give Christian alms" (Question 103). Calvin supported the commandment with the aid of disciplinary and police
power. But this is something which I would certainly not recom-
mend.

One thing, however, should be clear. No one who tries to play off
against each other religious service in ordinary life and religious serv-

ice as a special assembly of the congregation can appeal to Paul. On the contrary, Paul took for granted the congregational service and wrote about it only when—as in Corinth—there were conflicts. So I feel particularly encouraged here by Paul, who issues a strong warning against acclimatization and adaptation—literally "conformism" —to the trends prevailing in the world. Paul appeals to critical judgment, to reason, which of course needs renewal, precisely in order to test and distinguish in every situation and—when necessary—to dissociate oneself and to do so according to the supreme norm of the will of God, who wants what is good, pleasing, and perfect: "Do not be conformed to the structure of this world, but be transformed in a new mind, so as to be able to test what is God's will, that is what is good, pleasing, and perfect."

Crisis of Worship—Crisis of the Church

In this notorious crisis there is, of course, no simple and easy formula which avoids conformism while providing a positive justification of Sunday worship. Certainly the crisis is to a large extent the result of *developments in society* as a whole. Some things are clear.

In the drift to secularization and industrialization the former homogeneous society, under definite religious influences, has been largely dissolved. The influence of the churches in the political, economic, educational, and social fields has been restrained. Religious life and activity have long ceased to be taken for granted. Social pressure to attend church—apart from conditions in relatively compact Catholic villages and small towns—has in practice wholly disappeared. Sunday attendance at a religious service, formerly taken for granted, has become a private affair. Thus what was known as the Church of the people, the traditional Church, has been increasingly replaced by a Church of decision, demanding from each individual a personal reaction, a free decision of faith, and a free practice of faith. A numerical decline is understandable in these conditions, but it is only partly compensated by more deliberate and more decided faith.

Many, who acknowledge God and Jesus Christ in practical life, cannot make up their minds to attend a religious service regularly. And this fact alone shows that it is not merely the "wicked world" or secular society, unwilling to accept an invitation to a religious service, which is responsible for the crisis of worship. The very *churches* which invite people to come and worship are also responsible.

The reason is that they themselves appear so uninviting to many of our contemporaries—even our Christian contemporaries—so inhospitable, inhuman, and even unchristian.

I suggest as an example of a church which must seem uninviting the Catholic Church in West Germany, with which I am more familiar (there are certainly other examples). There we had a synod recently which closed after meeting over a number of years. The synod drew up a modern-sounding, wordy document on our hope, but never once took any bold step in response to the hopes which many in Germany and elsewhere had set on it. It did not offer

hope for married people tormented in conscience, who were expecting at least an unqualified approval of "artificial" birth control and a dissociation from the encyclical *Humanae Vitae;*

hope for divorced people who want to take part again in the eucharistic celebration;

hope for students of theology who feel called to parish ministry but not to celibacy (in the course of only three years from 1969 to 1972 there was a decline of about 60,000 candidates for the priesthood in the Catholic Church);

hope for priests who had to give up their ministry because of a legitimate marriage, many of whom would like to be recalled (this has meant a loss of more than 30,000 priests in the last ten years in the world as a whole and even now—according to information from Rome—an annual loss of 3,500 to 4,000 priests);

hope for parishes deprived of their priests to a rapidly increasing extent and having to make do with lay persons authorized to give Holy Communion, largely as a result of the law of celibacy, which is clearly contrary to human rights, expressly contradicts the words of Jesus and Paul, and goes against a practice maintained in the Catholic Church as a whole for its first thousand years;

hope for responsible people, priests and laity, in the dioceses, who expect to have some say in the choice of their bishops and are looking for a more democratic procedure to secure this (to say nothing of papal elections);

hope for all the people and the congregations in the different churches who want at last mutual recognition of church ministries and an open eucharistic fellowship, common building and common use of churches, and so on.

I hope that what I have said will not be taken in the wrong way and I would not like to give the impression that I am running down the synod. So many men and women boldly committed themselves and wanted to achieve so much more. But the majority of the bishops did not want more, because—and this is an open secret— Rome does not want more. Thus priests and parishes affected will be provoked to take measures to help themselves and thus unfortunately to further uncontrolled experiments, disorder, and polarization. But again we must ask: Is such a Church, talking so much about hope and doing so little to create it, likely to be effective in inviting people to its services? Is it not this unsympathetic, immobile, senile, blind institutional Church under which also many loyal churchgoers themselves suffer? Is it surprising if congregations are becoming smaller in such a Church, where claim and reality, talk and action, diverge so scandalously?

In view of this situation in society and Church, it is not easy to answer the question: "Worship today—why?" And I would not want to give the impression that one person had to answer this question on behalf of all the rest. It is for every serious Christian to begin again to consider thoroughly the question of the religious service. Here then are some ideas to provoke further reflection, at the same time assuming that today fulfillment of a commandment, consideration for the family, habit, and the need of fellowship no longer provide adequate motivation for attending a religious service. I would like to invite you to reflect on the opportunity which a religious service can offer even today: first for the individual, then for the community. Here then is a first, brief consideration.

For Man's Sake

Politicians and directors of industry, even scholars and busy people in all callings, in the midst of constant strain and stress, complain that they are unable to find time for reflection, to ask what is the point of it all, what are the real goals for which they are striving, what ought to be done in principle in one way or another. . . . Mentally we are living from hand to mouth.

We are slowly beginning to see, however, that in this efficiency-oriented consumer society man needs more than ever vacant areas, not occupied by his calling, not completely scheduled for work, where he is freed from the constraints of the industrial mass society; above all, he needs leisure periods, to be used intelligently. But it is just this intelligent use of free time which is by no means guaranteed —as we know—by the constantly expanding leisure-time industry: people can be landed in new constraints by an excessive supply of commercial aids to the use of leisure in the longer weekend.

Does not man need to find real repose also within the week-day rhythm, not merely externally by sleeping it off or simply doing nothing but also inwardly by true recuperation: to enable him to come to himself, to come to his senses, to orient himself to his proper goals and norms and thus catch up on himself and recuperate?

In this connection does not a well-conducted act of worship provide an irreplaceable opportunity for man (there will be something to be said later about its quality)? It is not God but man who gains by our worship. For man it means a great opportunity,

if in worship he can reactivate his living faith in God and in Christ, a faith that cannot by any means be taken for granted;

if he thus becomes once more calm and more composed, gets away for a while from the daily pressure and agitation;

if he is confronted with reliable exemplary values and can again orient himself to primary and ultimate standards;

if he realizes that he is bound to a truth;

if he discovers afresh and acquires afresh some meaning in his inconsistent life and in a still more inconsistent history of mankind.

And is it not of the greatest importance for a young person to be confronted with exemplary values, standards, and an ultimate horizon of meaning, particularly in a democratic system—an open libertarian-pluralistic system—which of its very nature cannot officially prescribe a *Weltanschauung,* designate in a doctrinaire fashion any supreme values or primary standards, or provide a universal definition of an ultimate meaning? Then he will not lose his bearings, go astray, break down, or despair, still less succumb to a totalitarian system of one color or another with a totalitarian prescription for his orientation.

A good religious service can again provide an ultimate orientation for all the innumerable, inescapable, relevant decisions of life: an orientation which does not abolish freedom but makes it possible in virtue of the commitment to the one true God.

A good *Christian* religious service, however, is a memory of Jesus Christ, continually reactivated by word and meal: a memory of Jesus of Nazareth, made—it is to be hoped—continually freshly alive in his whole visibility and audibility, the basic model to be realized in a variety of ways, inviting modern man to a new outlook on life and a new practice of life. Anyone who has experienced this can also testify to the fact that in this way the religious service can really produce for man in his ordinary life a wider horizon, a clearer line, a firmer conviction and also—to put it quite simply—a little more courage, joy, and freedom for the following week. But now we come to the second consideration.

For the Community's Sake

We do not live our Christian faith in isolation. There is no one who is not dependent on others. That is why the Christian message directs the believer into the community of believers: a community however which should not be self-centered, not an end in itself, but at the service of men. But how is a community to be active in the world, in modern society, if it never meets together? For what Jesus wanted should be realized fraternally, in a community.

It is through the religious service that a congregation is formed and continues to be formed afresh as a community of those who are convinced of Christ's cause and prepared to be his disciples: A Church is constituted. For our word "Church" is a translation of *ecclesia,* and *ecclesia* literally means "assembly." A crowd of Christians dispersed throughout the city, if they are more than merely baptized Christians, may amount to something really respectable. But such a mere agglomeration of Christian individuals is not an assembly, a congregation, an *ecclesia,* a Church.

It can be seen that the congregation and its worship are not optional supplements to being a Christian. They are a necessary precondition and at the same time the implementation and concretization of being a Christian: discipleship of Christ implemented and made concrete, to which the individual is in fact provoked but which also needs social realization.

In the concrete, then, what would being a Christian amount to if congregations and their worship were allowed to die? Certainly there can be Christian worship in the ordinary secular routine. But where and how are we to recall the source from which we emerged and from which we must constantly re-emerge if we are to remain Chris-

tians? Where are we to recall—thanking, praising, petitioning—the
words and deeds, the suffering, dying, and new life of this Jesus of
Nazareth, who for Christians must remain the Christ, the authoritative standard? Where, if not in proclamation, in prayer, in meditation, in the hymns and in the meal of the Christian religious service,
where at one and the same time we can look back to the source, look
forward to a better future, and expect a realistic initiation into the
present?

Objections

Should we take part in a religious service only when we feel *what is
described as a "need"*? But we may also ask: If we reduce everything
to the immediate satisfaction of a need, are we not ruining any sort
of friendship, love, marriage, any sort of fellowship, and in fact any
community? We have nothing to say against genuine human needs,
even in the religious field, although theologians have preached
against them far too frequently. Anyone will admit, however, that
there are superficial, short-term emotional needs which often arise
quite spontaneously. But there are also deeper, more comprehensive
needs of human life, of both body and mind, which can be
suppressed and of which man must occasionally also be reminded.

It is clear then that prayer and worship are not superfluous luxu-
ries but important and indeed necessary to life, something which
must not become stunted if we are to remain fully human, something
however which easily declines and even dies if it is not cultivated.
These things must not only be talked about but exemplified for children in the life of parents more convincingly than formerly when
Christianity and worship were still taken for granted.

Worship is not by any means merely a way of satisfying religious
needs, nor is it concerned merely with what is necessary or important
for human life. In the last resort—precisely because it is a service
of God, a "divine service"—worship involves something more than
man. It involves God himself. Quite apart from man's needs and
aims, apart from whatever is necessary or important, ought it not
to be truly appropriate, ought it not to be for him the most utterly
human thing, also simply and forthrightly to praise and extol his
God and Creator, to thank and supplicate him?

Any appeal to the Christian's freedom is irrelevant here. As we saw, when Luther and the Reformers spoke of Christian freedom, they meant something quite different. The Church of Jesus Christ is not a compulsory organization, it is a Church of voluntary members. Their voluntary membership, however, does not exclude but in fact includes obligations and ties voluntarily accepted. Any community which does not insist on a minimum of obligation and participation soon ceases to exist as a community. No community which wants to function internally and externally can be content with merely passive members.

All kinds of clubs and associations have the courage to insist on regular—often weekly—attendance and to some extent closely control this, without their voluntary members feeling that they are subject to compulsion or violence. Should not a Church then also have the courage to resist the quest for ease and comfort, however understandable, and expect and demand regular participation as something completely obvious, for the sake of the great common cause, for the sake of God and men? Only in this way can we in fact achieve that mutual encouragement in faith on which we are dependent as human beings living among other human beings.

This means for *Catholics:*
no legal "Sunday obligation," which has to be fulfilled on pain of "mortal sin." For too long we have instilled fear in people and driven them to church with threats of hell and the devil.

This means for *Protestants:*
no more passive acceptance of empty churches in Protestantism. For too long participation in worship (unlike the church tax[1]) has been left completely to the whim of the individual, as a result of a false conception of evangelical freedom. For too long silence has reigned on this obligation, because people lacked the courage of their convictions, when it ought to have been loudly proclaimed; or at most complaints have been aired internally when there ought to have been plain speaking in public.

But however the Protestant churches consider the matter—and they should reconsider it—I would like to hope that in my own church, the Catholic Church, we shall maintain clearly and unmistakably this obvious minimal obligation for the sake of human beings and congregations. We have rightly expressly abolished the precept of Friday abstinence, many obsolete devotions and customs, and long outdated commandments of the Church, or simply dropped them in practice—not least as a service to ecumenism. But regular worship—normally on Sunday or on Saturday evening, if necessary even on a weekday—is neither an antiquated custom nor a secondary matter. While making the most generous allowance for excusing causes in the individual case, anyone who wants to call himself a Catholic should be aware of the fact that in the future also regular participation in the religious service is the minimal obligation expected of him.

A Good Religious Service

Of course any obligation to Sunday worship becomes an insupportable burden whenever the service is carried out in a merely correct way and not well organized. From the time of the Second Vatican Council the Catholic liturgy has taken up and put into effect some of the essential demands of the Reformation. We hear again the word of God intelligibly proclaimed; all the people take an active part; the liturgy is adapted to different nationalities, simplified, concentrated, and clearly related to Jesus' last supper. Long disputed questions have been settled, at least in principle: Instead of Latin we now have the mother tongue, instead of private Masses a community celebration of the eucharist, and—at least in certain cases and in smaller groups—communion under both kinds.

In both Catholic and Protestant churches today it depends largely on the individual parish priest or pastor how good, how realistic, how closely related to the situation and how concentrated on the message of Jesus Christ the congregational service in his parish is. And fortunately, despite widespread formalism, ritualistic stereotypes, and excessive intellectualist boredom, we find everywhere today services with life, joy, spontaneity: in brief, services which are really celebrations, truly human festivals, stirred by the Spirit of Jesus Christ. And—this is one of the most gratifying signs of the Church's renewal—the way has been prepared for a new language and a new music which are finding expression in innumerable new prayers and hymns, often quite spontaneously emerging in parochial and student congregations, formulated frequently by young and completely unknown people, or even given shape spontaneously in the course of the service itself.

Unfortunately, not only in Rome but also in the Catholic Church in Germany and elsewhere reactionary trends are becoming stronger.

After a successful reform of the Scripture readings, measures are now being introduced, with the aid of a new missal, a uniform hymn book, and superfluous "people's missals" in preconciliar style, to suppress again all spontaneity in worship and to pin down the leaders of our congregations to such "aids" and to very high and hollow-sounding prayers. If we want a service as boring, sterile, and inopportune as possible, if we want to empty our churches still more and to repel young people still more, if we want to breed even more homogeneous and restricted congregations organized according to age, sociological structure, and mentality, even according to clothing and possessions, then we must keep as literally as possible to all these pseudomodern patterns of worship.

Certainly we do not want any irresponsible liturgical adventures or a chaotic liturgy. But neither do we want again a post-Tridentine regimentation, a regulated, high-flown language which leaves the liturgy frozen again for centuries. On the contrary, it must be clearly stated that, however much we want to maintain a firm basic shape and framework, particularly for the eucharistic celebration, not only place and time, ceremonies, vestments, and gestures but also forms of hymns and speech must be treated in principle not as constants but as variables in the service. And the leader of the congregation has not only the right but also the duty (obviously in connection with other congregations and with the whole Church) to look for forms suitable for his congregation and also for good texts. If the official texts and hymns are good, so much the better. But only the best prayers and hymns, wherever they may be found, are good enough for worship today. The criterion must be that they are covered by the Christian message itself and at the same time are completely intelligible for people today. This applies above all—but not only—to us Catholics.

I may be permitted, however, to speak frankly about one problem with which Protestants themselves are very much preoccupied: the neglect of the Lord's Supper in Protestant worship. Certainly being a Christian means the following of Christ in radically human action. Certainly the word should retain its priority in worship. Certainly the celebration of the meal may not take such a grandiose form as to suggest that carrying out the ritual is the most essential practice of the Church and participation in it the test of a person's Christianity.

But in practice the celebration of the eucharist in some Protestant churches today presents a very sad spectacle. Or is there any support in the New Testament or in the practice of the early Church for moving the Supper away from the center and making it more an appendage than a constitutive element of Christian worship? Is it permissible for the service of preaching largely to dominate Sundays and the eucharistic service to become an unusual, alien act of worship?

I have no wish to draw up a list of all that is lacking in a service thus reduced to the word. But, after the Catholic Church in recent years has given expression in its services to so many Protestant concerns and for some of its traditionalists has become more or less "Protestant," there should no longer be any fear on the Protestant side of being accused of "Catholicizing." There should be a resolute commitment to a revaluation of the Supper and thus to a more integrated, truly festal act of worship, making more demands on the individual, stressing the community, appealing more to sight and to imagination than to the intellect.

All this would only be to the advantage of the service of the word, where the congregation unfortunately is often active only in the singing and in saying the Our Father; it would be understood less intellectually, less subjectively, less individualistically or spiritualistically. For the service of preaching and the service of the meal are not alternatives. They are no more alternatives than are religious services as processes of learning or festive celebrations, with a large congregation or with a small group, with a fixed rite or freely organized.

Prospect

From the very beginning, Sunday for Christians was not merely a postponed Sabbath or a day of rest to be observed in a legalistic spirit but the resurrection day, the Lord's day, on which the Lord's Prayer was said standing and his supper celebrated in the spirit of a family meal.

I would like to invite conservatives and progressives, old and young, Catholics and Protestants to seize once again the opportunity offered for man in our time in the religious service and—it is to be hoped—ever more frequently in a common ecumenical eucharist. In the Catholic Church in the present century the efforts of many decades were needed to get the congregation actively participating in the liturgy of the word and particularly in the liturgy of the eucharist. But it was achieved once the effort had been made to achieve it.

Therefore let us renew our striving and now let it be a common effort.

A religious service—properly celebrated—can actually become that for which we all long: the feast of our liberation, the precelebration of our final redemption. Seen in this way, a religious service can provide us with a kind of leisure, a genuine free period: the necessary counterweight to working time and the world of achievement, to our ordinary routine; an intimation, a perception, an advance in faith and hope toward a new man, a new creation.

For two thousand years Christians have celebrated their religious service. Is it not to remain so in the future? Is it not to become so again? Rightly understood, the Sunday religious service will never be isolated from the working-day service of God but of itself will lead us into daily life. That is why for the Christian the week begins with Sunday, with Sunday worship as a promise for ordinary daily life and as a signpost to everyday life. *Oratio et actio,* prayer and action, Sunday and working day, attachment to the Church and attachment to the world: these things go together for the Christian and his worship, today more than ever.

Translated by EDWARD QUINN

NOTE

1. In Germany every professing Christian is bound by law to make a contribution to his own church (Catholic or Protestant) as part of his income tax. —*Translator.*

VI. What is Confirmation?

Introduction

For a long time theology has found it particularly difficult to cope with the sacrament of confirmation. Its origin is enigmatic, its rite variable, its interpretation inconsistent. Hence a *theological* meditation on confirmation cannot be entirely simple.

The numerous problems culminate in the question: Can there be a distinct sacrament for giving the Spirit, independent of baptism, although the latter also bestows the Holy Spirit? Confirmation seems to lack all the important elements of a sacrament: institution by Christ, a constant outward sign, a specific effect in addition to that of baptism, necessity for salvation; the minister too and his authority, the recipient and his age, are uncertain.

This uncertainty cannot be removed without recourse to the origins and to tradition. Without this appeal even today both new theological definitions and practical reforms will remain purely arbitrary and therefore unstable.

I explained concretely in *On Being a Christian* the general meaning of recourse to the origins. What is relevant to a first introduction to the Christian faith becomes clear from the first part of the present book, "On Being a Christian: Twenty Theses." It is impossible today to attach too much importance particularly to a good, introductory basic catechesis for our children if the "sacraments of initiation," the "introductory sacraments"—that is, baptism and confirmation—are to be meaningfully celebrated.

A piece of advice for the reader who has no special training in theology: If he finds less interesting the highly complicated biblical and historical problems expounded as briefly and concisely as possible in the first half of this meditation, he may well begin with the section on "The Bond of Confirmation with Baptism." On the other hand, anyone who would like more biblical and historical information on confirmation will find it in the book *Ein Sakrament des Geistempfangs?* by J. Amougou-Atangana.[1]

Tübingen, January 1976

A Separate Sacrament in the New Testament?

The basic evidence

In the whole of the New Testament there is not a single text, not a word or a sign of Jesus to suggest that he instituted a sacrament of confirmation. Nor does it seem that there are any indirect allusions which might imply such an institution.

In the whole of the New Testament—and this is particularly clear in Paul and John—the giving of the Spirit is linked with *baptism*. This is true also of Luke and his Acts of the Apostles (cf. 1:5, 2:38, 9:17–18, 11:16). The account of Pentecost in particular—presented as a baptism of the Spirit for the apostles—links the giving of the Spirit with baptism for the new believers; nowhere is there any mention of a laying on of hands, still less of a confirmation. Hence it is wrong to describe Pentecost—as some have done—as "primal confirmation."

Exceptions

As against this basic evidence there are two texts of Acts which have been used to attempt to substantiate the idea of an autonomous sacrament of confirmation. These appear to be *exceptions* and, precisely because of their irregularity, point to the *solidarity* of baptism and reception of the Spirit. According to both the account of the laying on of hands by the apostles in Samaria (8:14–17) and that of the disciples of John in Ephesus (19:1–7), a baptism which does not impart the Spirit is not really a true baptism but must be supplemented by reception of the Spirit. (According to the story of the centurion Cornelius and the reception of the Spirit by the Gentiles in Acts 10:44–48, on the other hand, the bestowal of the Spirit by God means that baptism cannot be refused to those so graced: Giving the Spirit and baptism go together.)

The historical obscurities and inconsistencies of both these exceptional texts are discussed at length by commentators: They can be understood only in the light of their purpose and from the whole theological conception of the Lucan Acts of the Apostles. (The works of E. Käsemann, H. Conzelmann, and E. Haenchen should be consulted on this topic.) In the interest of the unity of the Church, threatened by Gnostics and heretics, and of the continuity of salvation history Luke himself evidently recast the original narratives in such a way that they could be fitted into his theologically determined presentation of the history of the primitive community.

1. From among John's disciples who actually knew nothing of the Baptist's role as precursor or about the Spirit there emerged that singular type of Christian ("disciple," "believer") who was inconceivably ignorant of the very existence of the Spirit and who was then received into the apostolic Church by laying on of hands, so that he would not seem to be in competition with Jesus' disciples. (The same sort of thing appears in the recasting of the story of Apollos in Acts 18:24–28.)

2. The relatively independent Church of Samaria, where Philip had preached without express mandate, must have been received—after the apostles' visitation—into communion with the apostolic Church and with Jerusalem as the center of its unity: Only then, according to Luke, was the Spirit given. (The story of Cornelius is similarly theologically determined, the mission to the Gentiles being ascribed expressly to God's will as a result of the preceding bestowal of the Spirit.)

These texts, then, are related to the incorporation of ecclesiastical outsiders in Samaria and Ephesus into the one Church under the sovereignty of Jerusalem and of the circle of the Twelve. The point they make is not the idea of baptism but the idea of the Church, seen against the background of a history of salvation which—in the light of the Old Testament—is centered on Jerusalem and starts out at the midpoint of time from Jerusalem.

These two theologically intelligible but historically dubious texts then make a separation of baptism and the giving of the Spirit seem a priori illegitimate. In view of the unanimous evidence of the New Testament with reference to the unity of baptism and the giving of the Spirit, they cannot provide any basis for a separate sacrament of reception of the Spirit. Nor were they understood in this way in the early history of the Church.

A Separate Sacrament in the Ancient Church Tradition?

Second and third centuries

The complete silence of the sources with reference to a separate sacrament for giving the Spirit in the immediate subsequent period is explained in the light of the New Testament evidence. The tradition of the *second century* has no reference to an institution by Christ, nothing about a special sacrament of confirmation. In strict continuity with the New Testament, at this time too baptism of water and this alone is the sacrament of reception of the Spirit. The "seal of the Spirit" is granted by washing in water and not by a postbaptismal laying on of hands, of which we have no evidence at all in this century.

Only in the *third century* is there any mention—especially by Tertullian and Hippolytus—of rites in connection with baptism out of which the rite of confirmation was later constructed: laying on of hands, anointing, signing with the cross. In Rome there was even an odd second, postbaptismal anointing, the origin of which is obscure but which is of the utmost importance for the development of the later rite of confirmation. Nevertheless, it is begging the question to argue from the mere existence of these rites to an independent sacrament.

Neither Tertullian nor Hippolytus refers to the laying on of hands in the Acts of the Apostles. The first to do this is Cyprian, for whom, however, baptism of water still imparts the Spirit in his fullness and for whom there is no distinction between "baptized" and "confirmed." Apart from Cyprian's reference to laying on of hands to impart the Spirit, there is no evidence anywhere in the third century that anointing, laying on of hands, and signing—whether individually or in a total structure—accord a postbaptismal gift of the Spirit. Even the name *confirmatio* is not used in this connection before the third century.

late patristic times

Even in later patristic times, despite the expansion of the postbaptismal rites, if they are practiced at all, the Spirit continues to be given in baptism. The postbaptismal rites are carried out together with baptism and do not bestow any special gift or specific sacramental effect. This is true also for Ambrose, who at this time uses the term *confirmatio,* and for Jerome, who already witnesses to episcopal visitations with laying on of hands; it is true also for Augustine, who is responsible for the emphasis on the doctrine of original sin and therefore on infant baptism. The postbaptismal rites remain an integral part of baptism as the one and only sacrament of initiation. The theology of initiation remains essentially a theology of baptism.

Hence it is entirely understandable that there has been no separate rite of confirmation (only postbaptismal anointing, directly connected with baptism) in the *Eastern churches* up to the present time and consequently (apart from late adaptations to Western developments) no specific theology of confirmation. In the East the ancient tradition is maintained without more ado: The presbyter administers baptism together with the postbaptismal rites.

The Emergence of the Western Rite of Confirmation

The factual development

It is only in the Latin West that we find the detachment of the postbaptismal rites as a *separate development*—which at first occurs simply as a fact at different times and places—and consequently the emergence in practice of an independent rite; finally a theology of confirmation distinct from that of baptism is worked out to justify the development.

The decisive factor in the formation of a separate rite was the *prerogative of the bishops as ministers of the postbaptismal rites* which was claimed in practice in the West. (Behind the practice lay on the one hand the Augustinian theology of original sin and the necessity of baptism and on the other the now universal custom of infant baptism.) These rites were increasingly deferred. As a rule there was a demand for the child's baptism by the priest as soon as possible, but also for the postbaptismal rites to be carried out by the bishop as soon as possible: at first on the same day or at least in the same week. Soon, however, it came to depend on the accessibility of the bishop, and there might be a long delay. The bishop now came to those who had been baptized. (Here is the starting point for the later episcopal visitations mainly for confirmation.)

The prerogative of the bishops as ministers of the postbaptismal rites therefore did not presuppose, but in fact created, two independent sacraments. The splitting up of the rite of baptism was by no means regarded as normal at the beginning. For a long time the attempt continued to be made to enforce infant "confirmation" as quickly as possible after infant baptism—as was the practice in the East. It was only in the thirteenth century that opposition began to relax and allowance was made officially for the concrete situation. In 1280 a provincial council at Cologne postponed confirmation until at least the child's seventh year. A minimum instead of a maximum age was now required. But adults were to continue to follow the older tradition and to receive the postbaptismal rites immediately after baptism.

Originally the postbaptismal rites had been extremely simple more or less, like the anointing at baptism today. It was only from the ninth century that the odd second anointing (signing with chrism), which at first had been known only in Rome, was expanded to a self-contained "rite of confirmation." At the same time the opening and closing prayers, all of which are determined by the baptismal liturgy, provide the theological motifs for this rite which is still seen in connection with baptism but has now become autonomous.

Theological justification

What had been liturgical practice for a long time was finally given a theological ratification. It was only in the High Middle Ages that a specific theology was drafted to provide a subsequent justification of the now autonomous rite to be carried out only by the bishop: "confirmation theology." It attempted to define the difference—so difficult to explain—between this "confirmation" and baptism, the proper function, the necessity for salvation, and the sign of this separate rite.

This confirmation theology, significantly enough, takes a sermon as its starting point. In the homily *Advertamus* (attributed to Faustus of Riez) for the first time in theology a distinction between baptism and confirmation as two independent factors is made and justified. Regardless of the patristic tradition (this is important), it is now asserted that in confirmation the Christian is given strength to fight (confirmation is regarded as the armor of the soldier of Christ). It means an "increase of grace" for the present life. Only later did Amalric of Metz extend this grace to an "increase in glory" in the next life.

This still embryonic theology of confirmation, the product of practical developments, enters into the *Decretum Gratiani* (which forms the basis of all medieval canon law) as a series of canons falsely ascribed to various popes, in which confirmation—since it is reserved to the bishop—is treated as an even greater sacrament than baptism. Peter Lombard, on whose "Sentences" more commentaries were written than on any other theological work of the Middle Ages, follows the same line and describes confirmation as the gift of the Spirit "for strengthening" (*ad robur*—by contrast with the gift of the Spirit in baptism, *ad remissionem,* "for forgiveness"): a classical formula retained in the textbooks up to the present time, but without any foundation in the liturgy and theology of the first millennium.

Aquinas finally gives this confirmation theology its classical form by providing a speculative justification, clarification, and support for the separate rite as it actually emerged. He does this especially by using the analogy—hitherto unknown—of bodily life: In the spiritual life two sacraments must correspond to man's birth and growth to adult age; in virtue of two distinct indelible features (baptismal and confirmation character) there must be two independent sacraments with two different effects of grace (grace of baptism and of confirmation).

The medieval distinction of the two sacraments is then definitively established by the Council of Florence in the Decree for the Armenians (1439) and without further theological reflection, confirmed against Luther by the Council of Trent. In all this the difference between the two ordinary ministers of the sacrament (presbyter for baptism, bishop for confirmation) is emphasized.

The Indeterminate Character of the Western Rite of Confirmation

Matter

The "matter" of the sacrament of confirmation is indeterminate: It changes according to place and time. There is no continuity between the rite of laying on of hands in the Acts of the Apostles and the first records of episcopal laying on of hands in connection with baptism. The modern rite of confirmation is based originally not on the Acts of the Apostles but on the baptismal rites attested in Tertullian and Hippolytus (laying on of hands, anointing, and signing with the cross), so that subsequently a competition arose—which has not been clearly decided up to the present time—between laying on of hands and anointing (with signing).

1. The postbaptismal *laying on of hands* for the giving of the Spirit was completely unknown in the Eastern churches during the first centuries. The laying on of hands which turned up in the West in connection with baptism only in the third century could have been an extension of the right hand over all the baptized persons together (probably a prayer over the newly baptized), as it is found later and up to our own century. The Pontifical of Bishop Durandus (d. 1296), important in the subsequent period, requires the extension of both hands; in Rome however from the twelfth century a hand was laid individually on each candidate.

Now, however, at the very time when the postbaptismal rites were taking on an independent existence and becoming understood even in theological terms as confirmation, signing with chrism came to the fore as the essential gesture of confirmation; when Innocent VIII in the fifteenth century prescribes the Pontifical of Durandus for universal use, the laying on of hands disappears to give way to anointing. As it had been already for Aquinas, so too for the Council of Florence in 1439 (cf. DS 1317)—for Trent the decisive authority against Luther—anointing is the "matter" of confirmation. Reinterpreting the texts of the Acts of the Apostles, Aquinas asserted that the apostles themselves had anointed when laying on hands.

It is only in the eighteenth century that Benedict XIV attempts to solve the difficulty by a compromise which still has legal force in the Catholic Church at the present time. The individual laying on of hands is restored, but in such a way that the right hand is laid on the candidate's head during the signing with chrism; such a cumulative rite of course contradicts even formally the Acts of the Apostles (laying on of both hands). The frequent attempts subsequently to trace back the postbaptismal laying on of hands to the apostles are thus shown to be impossible. On this point there can be no question of a continuous tradition.

2. Liturgically, postbaptismal anointing is possibly older than the postbaptismal laying on of hands. Unlike the laying on of hands, it is found also in the East. In the West the development is determined by two factors: on the one hand by the specifically Roman practice of double anointing and its establishment in the non-Roman liturgy; on the other hand by the bishop's exclusive prerogative of giving that second anointing which becomes the nucleus of the independent rite.

In the High Middle Ages anointing appears as the sole essential matter. Nor does the reintroduction of individual laying on of hands in the eighteenth century mean that anointing is suppressed. The latter then has undoubtedly a continuity greater than that of the laying on of hands. On the other hand the anointing in particular is without any foundation in the New Testament. Anointing with the Spirit, mentioned in the New Testament, refers to baptism and is not an allusion to a separate giving of the Spirit. From all this we may conclude that the "matter" of confirmation cannot be unequivocally defined and certainly cannot—as traditional sacramental theory requires—be traced back to Jesus Christ.

Form

The "form" of the sacrament of confirmation is indeterminate. The formula already known to Aquinas but beginning to prevail universally only in the sixteenth century as a result of a papal decree says nothing about laying on of hands: *Signo te signo crucis, et confirmo te chrismate salutis, in nomine Patris et Filii et Spiritus Sancti* ("I sign you with the sign of the cross, and I confirm you with the chrism of salvation, in the name of the Father and of the Son and of the Holy Spirit"). In the Middle Ages people believed in the apostolic origin of this formula.

But the important expression *confirmo* entered comparatively late into the formula and, as a technical term of Roman origin, describes the postbaptismal rites as a whole. The formula does in fact go back to early patristic times. It does not, however, imply any special gift of the Spirit (there is nothing about strength, maturity, growth), but confirms indirectly the fact that the Spirit is received in baptism.

It can rightly be asked whether the formula was not originally simply the one used at the baptismal anointing. The homogeneous and yet surprisingly vague formula easily conceals the fact that the modern rite of confirmation is very much an agglomeration of a variety of competitive motifs and gestures. These have emerged by being detached from the baptismal context as a result of that episcopal prerogative of the second postbaptismal anointing, which then became increasingly emphasized in the formula in the course of time (*EGO signo*).

Effect

In such an indeterminate state of sacramental matter and form the specific *effect* of confirmation is also obviously indeterminate. Despite the most intense efforts, theologians have never hitherto succeeded in identifying a specific sacramental "grace" of confirmation which is unequivocally distinct from the effect of baptism. There are, indeed, numerous appellations and interpretations of confirmation, but, if they are not merely arbitrary, they all apply equally to baptism. "Completion," "seal," "armor of faith," "fullness of the Spirit" are used in the early Church not for a separate rite but for baptism of water as the initiation rite properly so called; a specific title for the supplementary rites—which vary with place and time and are carried out together with baptism—is superfluous.

The reservation of those terms for a "confirmation" detached from baptism, which stamps those who are "merely" baptized as "minors" in faith, became usual only from the Middle Ages onwards as the result of the above-described development. Even then it was not consistently observed and would have seemed a priori pointless in the centuries when adult baptism was the normal rule. The medieval theory of an independent "character" of confirmation therefore cannot appeal to the patristic conception of the *sphragis* (*signaculum*), since this refers to the "seal" of the Spirit who is given at baptism.

It is not however merely the conception of confirmation as sacrament of maturity, of coming of age, of initiation into adulthood, of manhood, of knighthood, which contradicts the early Church's understanding of baptism but also the definition likewise emerging in the Middle Ages of an autonomous sacrament additional to baptism, *ad robur:* for "strengthening" the Christian in his struggle against internal and external enemies, for the courageous public confession of faith, for martyrdom. All this the early Church linked with baptism. That Church would not have remained silent about a special sacrament for such purposes, particularly in times of persecution.

In recent times theologians have talked a lot about a specific sacrament of "the laity," "the universal priesthood," "lay ordination," "lay apostolate," "Catholic action," and other ideas of confirmation which would have been even less intelligible to the early Church. The fact that the lack of a criterion makes it possible to ascribe to one and the same sacrament of confirmation such a hotchpotch of different meanings and effects, which—apart from the very latest— could already be ascribed to baptism, strengthens the impression that what we have here is not an autonomous sacrament additional to baptism.

Age of the recipient

The age of the recipient of the sacrament of confirmation is indeterminate. In the East the postbaptismal rites are still carried out today at the same time as baptism: that is, normally for babies. In the West, at least officially, "confirmation" was predominantly for children under age up to the beginning of the thirteenth century.

After the Fourth Lateran Council in 1215, however, had implicitly approved the growing custom of postponing first communion to the age of reason, *ad annos discretionis* (seven to twelve years, or even fourteen to fifteen) (DS 812), the parallel tendency came to prevail officially also for confirmation. (The Provincial Council of Cologne

in 1280 made seven the minimum age, and this also found expression in the influential Catechism of the Council of Trent.)

In the nineteenth century, however, the custom arose in various
countries of confirming children not only at the age of twelve or
later, but also only *after* first communion. The decree of Pius X in
1910 on early communion, although it defined the age of reason
(*aetas discretionis*), strengthened the separation of baptism and
confirmation (cf. DS 3530–36). Yet again in the present century
there is a decided tendency to confirm before first communion and
thus to return to the ancient initiation sequence. The situation became more complicated as a result of Pius XII's decree on confirmation in 1946, once more permitting infant confirmation in cases of
necessity, so that children who would otherwise have died uncon-
firmed would not be deprived of the "increase of glory." In view
of these inconsistent developments, it seems impossible to suggest a
"normal age" for confirmation.

Minister

Finally, the minister of confirmation is also indeterminate. The
reservation to the bishop of the second postbaptismal anointing was
the reason for the postponement of confirmation and for its separation in time and place from baptism. In this sense it is possible to
understand the emphasis with which the Councils of Florence and
Trent define the bishop and him alone as the ordinary minister
(*minister ordinarius*).

But the decree of 1946 on confirmation, which assigns to all parish
priests and their representatives the power to confirm in case of necessity, again raises the question (constantly discussed) whether the
episcopal prerogative of confirming is merely a matter of canon law
(and therefore not a "divine right") and whether consequently every
priest might in principle possess the power to confirm (even if it is a
potestas ligata, a power whose use is restricted by law). Consideration of the practice of the Eastern churches (and of individual
cases also in the early Latin Church) enabled Vatican II to correct
the proposition declared anathema at Trent (DS 1777): The bishop
is now described not as *minister ordinarius* but as *minister origi-
narius* (original minister) of confirmation, so that the presbyter too
can be the *ordinary* minister of confirmation (Constitution on the
Church, art. 26). Furthermore Vatican II corrected the apodictic
Tridentine definition of the triple order of ministries, consisting of
bishops, presbyters, deacons, traced back to a "divine ordinance"

(DS 1777, cf. 1768), making it historically conditioned: "from antiquity" (art. 28).

The historical and exegetical findings lead to the inescapable conclusion that *episcopoi* and *presbyteroi* in the New Testament are either distinguished in a different way or not distinguished at all. The triple order of ministries is not found in the New Testament but is mentioned for the first time by Ignatius of Antioch and is, therefore, the result of a historical development which first took place in the region of Syria. There is no apparent distinction in principle between episcopal and presbyteral ordination. The modern bishop is undoubtedly distinguished from the presbyter by the fact that he presides over a wider ecclesiastical area. A canonical and disciplinary delimitation is possible and reasonable; a theological and dogmatic delimitation, on the other hand, is unjustified and impossible. The episcopal prerogative of confirmation, therefore—as the early Church well knew—is purely a question of canon law.

Thus in our time the end has caught up with the beginning. Progress in theology and in the Church has finally shown up the dubiousness of that development which lead to the cleavage between "confirmation" and baptism with all its consequences for "matter," "form," "effect," "minister," and "recipient." Thus the way is definitively free for fresh thinking and perhaps also for a new arrangement.

If we are finally to reach a theologically precise, consistent, convincing solution of the difficulties with which we have been burdened for so long, then the exegetical and historical findings briefly mentioned here must be taken seriously and made fruitful in theory and practice, not again patched over to serve the purposes of apologetics. A variety of insights will then emerge which can be stated here only in an abbreviated form. For the positive solution the reader must again be referred to the book by J. Amougou-Atangana,[2] which goes into detail on the problems merely touched on here.

The Bond of Confirmation with Baptism

Not an independent sacrament

The basic insight which emerges from the exegetical and historical findings is that *the modern rite of confirmation has been developed out of the baptismal rite.* The rite of confirmation is historically and substantially a part, an element, a phase of the one initiation which was accomplished in the Church from the very beginning with baptism. Without baptism there is no confirmation. But on the other hand—even according to completely traditional teaching—baptism is possible without confirmation. And also according to traditional teaching confirmation is not necessary for the salvation of the individual Christian.

If then confirmation is to make sense even today—a matter still to be discussed—it can only be *in close connection with baptism:* as linked with baptism, in explicating, confirming, and completing baptism. If the connection with baptism is overlooked, the interpretation and practical arrangement of confirmation will be left to the whim of the moment, as the various medieval and contemporary interpretations and attempts at reform abundantly prove. But theological theory and pastoral practice should be absolutely consistent.

Confirmation therefore cannot in any case be understood as an absolutely separate sacrament. It is *not an autarchic and autonomous sacrament,* independent of baptism. It simply cannot be put on the same plane as baptism. For this there is no support in the New Testament, nor can it clearly be seen to be connected with Jesus' proclamation and work; neither the outward sign nor the content and import of confirmation are so clear and determinate as to justify its equivalent status. Despite Luther's questioning, no one at Trent was yet aware of the complexities of the exegetical and historical evidence. But if its original connection with baptism is appreciated, the question of an institution of confirmation by Christ is automatically settled. At the same time the analogical (if not equivocal) character of the term "sacrament" as used at Trent again becomes clear. It is therefore possible to differentiate between confirmation and baptism (which, together with the eucharist, is the main sacrament) by calling the former a secondary sacrament which has a part in baptism.

As against the distinction, sometimes used as a way out, "baptism in Christ—confirmation in the Spirit," and similar *artificial distinctions,* it must therefore be stated emphatically that in both baptism and confirmation one and the same Christ is involved, one and the same Spirit, one and the same grace, and also one and the same faith.

Before the eucharist

If, then, confirmation is to have any meaning, it can only be as the *closing phase of the one rite of initiation.* Which means that it must be connected as clearly as possible and also chronologically with baptism and in any case *before admission to the eucharist.* Admission to the eucharistic feast and membership in the eucharistic community presupposes initiation, whether in one phase or in two. For historical, practical, and pastoral reasons that sequence alone is defensible which was maintained up to the nineteenth century: baptism, confirmation, eucharist.

No one who wants to uphold a sound, coherent relationship between theory and practice can at first assert the connection in theory between baptism and confirmation (confirmation as the closing phase and completion of initiation) and then determine arbitrarily the sacramental sequence, thus denying the connection in practice. If the eucharist is a sacrament for those already initiated—which no one denies—and if on the other hand confirmation is part of initiation—which seems irrefutable—then it is not logical to carry out confirmation only after reception of the eucharist.

It must not however be assumed that the *full significance* of confirmation is obvious or that it does not need to be reconsidered in the light of present-day circumstances. If today as formerly *adult baptism* were the normal rule, the problem would be stated differently. There would then scarcely be any reason for separating baptism itself from certain postbaptismal rites: Initiation might then be accomplished in a single act, as in the early Church or even today in the Eastern churches. It would be the same if ever the churches were to abandon child baptism in the sense of infant baptism and decide on child baptism in a broader sense (in the first years of school) or on adult baptism properly so called. But, at least for the present, this seems unlikely. In any case we should not be in too great a hurry to solve the problems of the day after tomorrow if we cannot yet see beyond those of today.

It will therefore be a good thing to consider confirmation today on the assumption that *child baptism* in the strict sense (infant baptism) will continue—despite all the criticism—to be the general practice in the main churches. This approach seems convenient also in the light of history. The development in the Eastern churches clearly shows that child baptism does not necessarily lead to the postbaptismal rites being carried out independently. But this *could* follow from child baptism and did so when the bishops reserved certain rites to themselves. The reason for the autonomy of confirmation was the reserva-

tion of these rites to the bishops. But it was child baptism which was
behind the reservation.

Child Baptism as Incomplete Baptism

Questionable child baptism

As with the Anabaptists at the time of the Reformation, so also
today (especially after Karl Barth's criticism) it is rightly felt that
there is something *questionable* about child baptism. For infants
would appear to lack the very thing which is a *conditio sine qua non*
for baptism: the act of faith. Someone who is incapable of hearing
the word is also incapable of responding to it in faith. The demand
for faith as an active response is connected with the demand for a
Church composed of voluntary members (as opposed to a "people's
Church," to which one belongs simply by accident of birth).

The scholastic theory of the infusion of an unconscious habit of
faith and Luther's idea of the faith of children are not convincing as
arguments against the demand for a free response of faith but are
merely hypotheses which can scarcely be proved.

The dispute cannot be settled in the light of the New Testament. It
is true that the baptism of whole "households" (or families), mentioned there, may have included baptism of children (analogous to
the baptism—or ritual bath—and circumcision of Jewish proselytes).
But nowhere in the whole of the New Testament is a child baptism
arranged or even merely mentioned. First Corinthians 7:14 describes
the children of Christian parents as "holy" merely in virtue of this
parentage, without any mention of baptism: This seems at best to
leave the question of child baptism for the children of converts open.
Only with the emphasis on infant baptism at the end of the second
century—it is argued—was there any pressure for the baptism of
children. In the light of the New Testament, of course, the decisive
question is not whether there were in fact child baptisms at that time
but whether any reason is given in this source to justify the practice.

For a long time it has been claimed that unbaptized children are
not saved, but this is a *false argument*. There is no uniform tradition
on the subject in the Church. Neither the Greek Fathers as a whole
nor the early Latin Fathers show any awareness of a "limbo" for
children but are more inclined to the view that they are saved even
without baptism. It was only Augustine at a later stage, as a result of

his controversy with Pelagius and his novel doctrine of original sin, who condemned unbaptized children to hell. From the early Middle Ages onward—especially from Anselm to Aquinas—this rigorous theory was increasingly modified: Hell was turned into a forecourt of hell and finally the forecourt of hell was turned into a forecourt of heaven, where the child enjoyed "Natural" bliss but not the vision of God. Today the idea of limbo is largely rejected, being regarded as a mere face-saving solution, without any foundation in the New Testament and contrary to God's universal salvific will. In the light of the revision of the Augustinian theory of original sin, it is also generally assumed that even unbaptized children have an opportunity of salvation.

Abolition of child baptism?

The abolition of child baptism would be bound to create *considerable difficulties* which, in the light of a very weighty, fifteen-hundred-year-old tradition of both Eastern and Western Christendom, cannot lightly be dismissed.

1. Postponement of baptism to adult age would obscure the fundamental significance of baptism for the Christian life and the community and emphasize instead personal faith and reflection.

2. The point of time at which a young person's faith is adequate to justify baptism would be hard to define in practice and would nevertheless again lead to some kind of general ruling. Presumably we would have to leave it to the psychologists to decide whether someone has sufficient faith at seven or only at thirty.

3. A once-and-for-all decision for baptism, made in the light of faith, like that of the early Christians, presupposes a specific conversion situation which would seem rather artificial in a society which is still outwardly Christian. Even today, in families which still bear (more or less) the stamp of Christianity, becoming a Christian is not the result of deliberately taking a new turning, but a gradual transition from a dependent, unconsidered faith to one that is independent and personal.

4. If adult baptism were the normal rule, a large number of churchgoers—unbaptized young people who would really be pagans —would have to be excluded perhaps for ten years or more, if not from the church service as such, at least from the heart of Christian worship, from participation in the eucharistic meal. They would be second-class worshipers in a Church which from the beginning

sought to be essentially a table fellowship. The inconvenience of this situation—for instance, in Baptist congregations—has led in some places to the creation of a substitute rite for child baptism (a consecration or something of the kind). But this again means losing sight of baptism as the basic sacrament, the sacrament of Christian initiation.

5. The attitude prevailing in a Christian community, where children were baptized as a matter of course, was therefore not the only reason why the demand for adult baptism as the sole legitimate form of baptism could not be made effective in the churches.

Justification of child baptism

Child baptism, supported by good reasons, *cannot be shown to be unjustifiable* from the outset in the light of the New Testament. It is usual to point to three aspects of the problem which in fact are to be understood as three elements of a single answer.

1. *God's gracious call precedes man's faith.* Child baptism witnesses to the fact that this small being is already in God's hands, that God has called it to salvation, and that the decision of faith can be understood only as a response to God's action.

2. *The child is not alone but is in vital contact with its family.* Child baptism gives expression to the fact that children belong to their parents also in a spiritual respect and are thus called with them to the same goal and already "sanctified." The Church baptizes children not in the abstract nor as individuals, for their own sake, but as sons and daughters of these Christian parents (which means also of course that practical conclusions must be drawn with regard to the will, the preparation, and the readiness of the parents for their children's Christian education).

3. *Child baptism destines the baptized person to faith and the profession of faith.* Child baptism expresses the essential solidarity of faith and baptism—which does not mean that they necessarily coincide in time. It does so because baptism marks out a person for faith, directs him to faith, and awaits his response in faith. God's Yes to man demands man's Yes to God. If the believer does not absorb the significance of baptism, child baptism remains fruitless. Only when the believer seizes on the meaning of baptism does child baptism reach its goal. Up to this point the parents (the godparents only secondarily)—who want baptism for the child, make the profession of faith, and promise a Christian education—are the representatives

of the child, so that at least in this sense there is a certain coincidence between (vicarious) faith and baptism. But only when the baptized person himself accepts the baptism which his parents wanted for him does baptism reach that integrity and completeness which is proper to adult baptism.

Uncompleted child baptism

From all this it follows that, even if child baptism can be justified in principle in the light of the New Testament and if in practice it is the solution to be preferred, it is by no means the ideal type of baptism envisaged by the New Testament. Even though it is in fact the normal case, in theological terms it remains a borderline case. Without faith actually realized, child baptism remains a torso: a kind of civic right in the community, truly granted but not claimed. Child baptism is therefore a *deficient mode of baptism:* an inconclusive, uncompleted baptism which calls for a conclusion, a completion, in actual faith and profession of faith on the part of the baptized person himself. And this is the very point at which confirmation could have its place and meaning in the light of both tradition and the actual situation.

The Meaning of Confirmation

Connection with baptism

Historically and essentially the significance of confirmation lies quite clearly in the fact that it renders explicit what is implicit in baptism, that it is a ratification and completion of baptism. Phenomenologically confirmation marks the point, within what is naturally a long and complex development, at which the child, baptized at the request and with the guarantee of his parents, after a basic catechesis suited to his age, publicly accepts his baptism and makes his profession of faith before the congregation. In this special rite he is recognized and accepted as a full member of the ecclesial community by its representatives, in order to be admitted to its eucharistic meal. Confirmation and first communion should take place in the same celebration.

Understood in this way, confirmation secures the basic link with baptism and has nevertheless its own significance and function as compared with baptism (child baptism). Baptism is not thereby emptied of meaning, nor is confirmation rendered superfluous. What happens is that the notorious fundamental deficiencies of child baptism are remedied and confirmation is given an unambiguous content.

The *call of God,* proclaimed for the child at baptism, is now consciously accepted and publicly answered by the young person himself.

The *faith* which the parents as representatives anticipated and which was merely called for and expected at the child's baptism now really exists as an affirmative, publicly professed, fully responsible decision on the part of the young person to direct his life in accordance with the standard of the gospel of Jesus Christ.

Baptism, at first received only passively by the child, now becomes effective as a result of the young person's actively grasping the offer of grace with explicit faith, with the profession of faith and with action in the light of faith.

The *Spirit,* granted at baptism as effective power, now becomes an existential reality, determining the young person's faith and life.

Reception into the Church, assured in principle to the infant and given formal expression in baptism, is now solemnly ratified with the publicly declared agreement of the young person and made concrete by his admission to the eucharistic meal. (The canonical effects in regard to membership of the Church, the rights and duties arising from it, ought to be reconsidered in this light.)

CON-firmation

This approach avoids a medieval, objectivistic sacramentalism which expects from a specific "grace of confirmation" wonderful results in this or the "next" life and for this reason demands confirmation even for infants. At the same time it overcomes that rationalist, subjectivist intellectualism which moralizes about confirmation, seeing in it mainly the conclusion of a course of instruction (Sunday school, moral instruction) and something like a rite of coming of age as a citizen or a Christian initiation into adulthood and a virtuous life. With confirmation therefore, as with baptism itself, the "objective" aspect (the actual pledge of salvation as the event of the Spirit) and the "subjective" aspect (man's response) must always be seen together. In connection with baptism confirmation is correctly understood only if we see in it the personal appropriation of the event of the Spirit.

In this synthetic (objective-subjective) view, provided we take into account a number of traditional elements, the term itself—"confirmation"—can be better understood

1. as ("subjective") *ratification* of the faith to which baptism commits him and which is now accepted by the baptized person on his own responsibility and as an obligation freely undertaken and publicly professed before the congregation;

2. as ("objective") *strengthening* of the baptized person, now believing and publicly professing his faith, by the Holy Spirit, received in baptism and becoming effective in actual faith.

The essence of confirmation

It should now have become more clear what was meant by defining confirmation as the explication, ratification, and completion of the event of the Spirit in baptism.

1. *Explication:* Confirmation is not an autonomous sacrament additional to baptism.

Historically and essentially it is a *continuation* and *explication* of baptism, the closing phase of baptismal initiation. That is why, like baptism, it cannot be repeated. The reason for this is not a sacramental "character of confirmation," but simply the fact that it shares in baptism and in the latter's unrepeatability.

2. *Ratification:* As explication of baptism, confirmation is not a complement, a repetition, still less a surpassing of baptism, as if the latter as such were imperfect.

It is in fact a *recognition* and *endorsement* of the baptism that has taken place. God's call *has* gone out, the Spirit *has* been granted, the baptism is valid, and the reception into the ecclesial community irrevocable; and to all this the baptismal recipient utters freely and publicly his Yes and Amen.

3. *Completion:* As explication and ratification of baptism, therefore, confirmation is not merely a formal ceremony of recognition or a bureaucratic reception procedure.

It is a *renewal* of the event of the Spirit at baptism, now becoming effective in deliberate acceptance, in actual faith, in public acknowledgment, and as such it is the final stage of *laying the foundations* of a Christian existence which is proved in discipleship. It is a completion therefore with reference to both the baptismal event itself and the faith which definitively and publicly lays hold on that event. Such a completion can only be the beginning and not the end of that

Christian life which, even after confirmation, is imperiled by weakness, doubt, temptation, unbelief, but which—despite all hazards—can be lived in the power of the Spirit of Jesus Christ.

The Practice of Confirmation

Explicit reference to baptism

This historically and theologically grounded link between confirmation and baptism must find expression also in the way the rite is carried out in practice. The following points should be considered.

Repetition of certain formulas from child baptism which adults and children can understand: in particular, the repetition of baptismal questions and answers and of a simple profession of faith directed toward the following of Christ (renewal of baptismal vows).

During confirmation the parents should stand at the side of their children; the godparents at baptism should also be the godparents at confirmation.

The reference—required by baptism—to the practice of the Christian life (indicative–imperative, gift–task, reception of the Spirit–living spiritually) ought to mark the whole rite of confirmation: It should be a concrete initiation into living discipleship of Jesus Christ.

Age

Suggestions about the right age for confirmation vary from one year to thirty years. The reason why this question creates so much disagreement is that the theological premises have not hitherto been clarified, while the attempt has been made to replace theological arguments with dogmatic (medieval or modern) prejudices, psychological and educational arguments, personal feelings, and subjective opinions. There must obviously be some scope for pastoral judgment on the age for confirmation. But, if theory and practice are not to come into conflict, a number of points must be considered.

1. *No infant confirmation:* The objections to infant baptism can be urged even more strongly against infant confirmation, since the deficiencies of infant baptism are aggravated by the deficiencies of infant confirmation. At the same time infant confirmation would give the impression—without theoretical justification—that it was necessary for salvation or for an "increase" in "grace" or in heavenly

glory. This is not to condemn the Eastern practice, since there the postbaptismal anointing carried out together with baptism never from the very outset had the significance of a separate, independent sacrament (with its own, specifically distinct "grace," in the Latin sense).

2. *Confirmation before admission to the eucharist:* This follows quite clearly from all that has been said about the consistency of theology and practice and about confirmation as the final phase of baptismal initiation, the latter being oriented for its own part toward admission to the eucharist as its goal. The link with baptism suggests that confirmation should follow as soon as possible after baptism and in any case before admission to the eucharist. If confirmation loses its link with baptism and its orientation to the eucharist, then in practice the age for confirmation will be arbitrarily decreed and of course in each case be provided with an ideological substructure. So at puberty it could be called the "sacrament of maturity"; at the attainment of legal majority, the "sacrament of adulthood"; or it might be postponed to the change of life, to the menopause, and be given the title of "sacrament of full maturity"; it might even be given at pensionable age as "sacrament of retirement"; or perhaps finally at the hour of death, when it would be the "sacrament of perseverance." Our exposition should have shown that all these attempts amount to pseudo solutions from the theological standpoint. And even in terms of educational psychology no one of them is better grounded than any other. On this subject it is not enough to quote our own opinions: We must produce solidly reasoned arguments.

3. *Psychologically, educationally, and pastorally, puberty and adolescence scarcely provide suitable conditions for confirmation:* The very concrete problems can be summed up under a few headings: awakening of sexual feeling; turning inwards (experience of self-awareness); dissenting attitude (phase of defiance, conflict experience) toward external authorities (home, school, Church); interiorization of religious feelings and aversion to professions of religion and to formal rites; overstrain arising from the need to make major decisions for life in regard to one's calling or further education, marriage, and family (often connected with a change of locality); pastoral difficulties in face of greatly fluctuating personal views; exclusion in practice of a large number of young people from confirmation and hence the danger of two classes of Christians; and

so on. In this connection what must be considered are not only the anxieties and negative experiences of our pastors with "Christian doctrine" as it used to be (something like this would still be necessary as preparation for confirmation), but especially the spiritual impoverishment resulting in Protestant circles from the postponement of confirmation to puberty. Admission to the eucharistic meal comes too late, the baptized person is not incorporated into the congregation, and the result is a largely unchurched Christianity. (Confirmation comes to mean confirming out of the Church.)

4. The most appropriate time for confirmation would seem to be *during the early years at school (before admission to the eucharist)*: This would seem to be suggested not only by the link in theological terms and the connection in time between confirmation and baptism but also by considerations of development psychology. At this time the child is already capable of learning in his own way what it means to be a Christian. This is a phase of still uncomplicated frankness, when the child is highly sensitive to religious ideas, open to a widening of knowledge, particularly ready to bear witness, to give an example, and to act decisively. In the New Testament the child—in his own way a complete human being, as development psychology stresses today—becomes almost a model of the attitude of faith.

The necessity of a basic catechesis suited to the child's age

The child can live into his faith (for it is not merely a question of a once-and-for-all decision) only if the Christian message is brought home to him in the right way, in a way suited to his mentality. As psychoanalysis makes clear, the parents themselves, their approach, and their whole behavior leave their mark on the child from the earliest years. On the other hand, in the conditions mentioned above, the function of a children's catechesis would be to provide a didactic introduction, giving scope for reflection, to what is meant by being a Christian.

The old-style, isolated instruction for confession and communion would not be desirable here. Nor is there any question of a theoretical study, memorizing and repeating "articles of faith." There must be a basic catechesis, rooted in the New Testament and at the same time related to the child's background and to practice, using the diverse modern educational methods and media to convey to the child what man's way is, what God and Jesus mean for his life, how in following Jesus Christ, always sustained by God and helpful to his fellow men, he can live and act, but also suffer and die, in a truly human way.

After one or two years of the basic catechesis the child would then been prepared definitively and publicly to accept the cause of Jesus, in order to be received as a full member into the ecclesial community and to be admitted to its eucharistic meal. "First communion" would then have to follow immediately on confirmation.

New shaping of the rite

The competition between laying on of hands and anointing, as already mentioned, went on for centuries. All we need say at this stage is that in any new shaping of the rite the laying on of hands is to be preferred, without necessarily excluding the anointing. The gesture of laying on of hands was taken over from the Old Testament (Moses is described as using it in Numbers 27:18–23) into the New, among other things, for ordination: Together with the intercessory prayer it is the visible sign of calling down the Holy Spirit on man. It is thus wholly in accordance with our understanding of confirmation as an explication, ratification, and completion of baptism and is completely intelligible even today. At the same time—the well-known passages in the Acts of the Apostles are relevant here—it gives expression to the ecclesial dimension: the definitively recognized acceptance into the Christian community. Compared with this, anointing (with simultaneous signing) might fall into the background or be reserved solely for the baptismal rite.

The *formula* accompanying the laying on of hands ought to express clearly the meaning of confirmation and especially its link with baptism (for example, "Receive in the Holy Spirit the completion of your baptism and, with faith in Jesus Christ, be a loyal member of his community"). The confirmand's previous profession of faith would have to be regarded as an integral part of the rite.

For the rest, the rite of confirmation must be *cleansed* from any remaining unbiblical, historically outdated, and unreal elements. Among these are certain theologically problematic or simply meaningless prayers and formulas and also a number of supplementary rites, like the blow on the cheek with which we had been burdened since the thirteenth century but which has at last been abolished. (It arose from Germanic symbolism and was meant to imprint impor-

tant events and facts—in this case the unrepeatability of confirmation—on the memory; originally it had nothing to do with a modified
kiss of peace or the conferring of a spiritual knighthood.) Moreover,
the laying on of one hand, which emerged from a cumulative process, combined with anointing and signing, ought to be replaced by
laying on of both hands. Finally, new canonical regulations should
exclude or correct such ideas as that of spiritual relationship between
godparent and godchild which have been linked traditionally with
confirmation.[3]

The minister

As we have seen, the question of the minister is not in principle
dogmatic but only a matter of pastoral expediency and of the corresponding canonical regulations.

Unfortunately, in many places the bishop is engaged often for
weeks at a time in traveling around the diocese for confirmations;
elsewhere the time of visitation of a parish is largely occupied with
confirmations. The result is that he is held back from more important
duties, from pastoral care for the pastors and from a thorough visitation of the parishes, so that "contact with the people" becomes
largely an illusion.

Because of the importance of a proper understanding of the rite of
confirmation and of its place in the Church as a whole (incorporation is not only into the local congregation but into the Church of
the one city, region, diocese), confirmation should not normally be
administered by whoever happens to be parish priest at the time. The
confirmand must be made vividly aware of the Church as extending
beyond the limits of his own parish.

Generally, therefore, the most suitable minister of confirmation
will be someone in a position midway between the diocesan bishop
and the local parish priest, someone who exercises both liturgical and
pastoral functions. The unsatisfactory arrangement with auxiliary
bishops residing in the cathedral city might well be replaced by that
of the early Church, with local bishops in each regional center to co-
ordinate the pastoral ministry of the region (or the city parishes)
and to carry out certain liturgical functions, under the leadership of
the diocesan bishop (= metropolitan). Confirmation might then be
administered annually by this local bishop. In the present situation,
in most dioceses, the deans would seem to have the appropriate sta-

tus for carrying out this task. But, whatever happens, it is very important to make the celebration (of confirmation and first communion) a truly festive occasion.

*   *   *

In this meditation the attempt has been made to work out consistently a theological definition of confirmation in terms of its function. It may be open to question on points of detail, but as a whole—we hope—it is based on solid exegetical and historical foundations. It is presented
with respect for the decisive, constant elements of the great Catholic tradition,
in response to the critical objections of the Reformation,
with a view to theologically justified practical solutions in the Church at the present time.

Translated by EDWARD QUINN

NOTES

1. In this short meditation only a few themes could be formulated and interpreted and the whole treatment might seem far too brief to anyone familiar with the complex exegetical, historical, systematic, and practical problems. It is based however on my lectures on the sacraments in Tübingen (winter term 1964–65, summer term 1967, summer term 1969), in the Protestant theological faculty of the University of Basel (summer term 1969), and at Princeton Theological Seminary (spring 1970). All these were recapitulated in a lecture given in Olten June 14, 1969, before the diocesan council of the diocese of Basel. This lecture was printed and first published in the *Theologische Quartalschrift,* vol. 153 (1974), pp. 26–47.
The complex problems have been thoroughly studied exegetically, historically, and systematically and independently expounded by a student of mine, J. Amougou-Atangana, *Ein Sakrament des Geistempfangs? Zum Verhältnis von Taufe und Firmung* [A Sacrament of Reception of the Spirit? The Relationship Between Baptism and Confirmation], Freiburg/Basel/Vienna, 1974. The reader in search of documentation, bibliographies, and detailed arguments may be referred to this book. It has enabled me to deal with these themes especially with greater historical exactitude.
I am particularly grateful to Karl-Josef Kuschel, my assistant in the

Institute for Ecumenical Studies, for his assistance in preparing this theological meditation for publication.

2. J. Amougou-Atangana, *op. cit.*

3. It should be noted that only the spiritual relationship arising from baptism constitutes an impediment to matrimony. In confirmation it involves solely a certain care on the part of the godparent and responsibility for the latter's Christian education. See Canons 797, 1079. —*Translator.*